D0284594

# THE COOK'S HERB GARDEN

Jeff Cox & Marie-Pierre Moine

**DK**

London, New York, Melbourne, Munich, and Delhi

**Editors** Helena Caldon,
Constance Novis
**Photographers** William Reavell,
Peter Anderson, Sarah Ashun
**Project Editor** Andrew Roff
**US Editors** Rebecca Warren,
Shannon Beatty
**Project Designer** Will Hicks
**Designer** Elly King
**Managing Editors** Dawn Henderson,
Angela Wilkes
**Managing Art Editor** Christine Keilty
**Senior Jacket Creative** Nicola Powling
**Senior Production Editor** Jennifer Murray
**Senior Production Controller** Seyhan Esen
**Creative Technical Support** Sonia Charbonnier

First American Edition, 2010

Published in the United States
by DK Publishing
375 Hudson Street
New York, New York 10014

10 11 12   10 9 8 7 6 5 4 3

176546—March 2010

Copyright © 2010 Dorling Kindersley Limited
All rights reserved

Without limiting the rights under copyright reserved above,
no part of this publication may be reproduced, stored
in or introduced into a retrieval system, or transmitted,
in any form, or by any means (electronic, mechanical,
photocopying, recording, or otherwise), without the prior
written permission of both the copyright owner
and the above publisher of this book.

Published in Great Britain
by Dorling Kindersley Limited.

A catalog record for this book is available from
the Library of Congress.

ISBN 978-0-7566-5869-4

DK books are available at special discounts when purchased
in bulk for sales promotions, premiums, fund-raising, or
educational use. For details, contact: DK Publishing Special
Markets, 375 Hudson Street, New York, New York 10014
or SpecialSales@dk.com.

Color reproduction by Colourscan, Singapore
Printed and bound in China by Hing Hung Printing

Discover more at
www.dk.com

*DK would like to thank
Petersham Nurseries
for their beautiful planted
pots and baskets.*

www.petershamnurseries.com

# CONTENTS

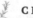

## A NOTE FROM THE GARDENER JEFF COX

I always think of culinary herbs as the champions of the kitchen garden. Their volatile oils—so attractive in teas and as flavors in our cooking—evolved as compounds plants use to defend themselves from insects and fungi. Both cooks and gardeners therefore benefit from an herb's aromas, because you don't need to use environmentally disruptive chemicals to protect them.

As I work and live with herbs, I befriend them. The familiar perennials return year after year to greet me with each warming spring; while the new annual acquaintances, which need sowing every year, unfurl from their tiny seeds into replicas of herbs from last year. Every year and throughout the seasons, the herb garden returns this friendship with a feast for all the senses.

In my garden, in the mild climate of Sonoma County, California, I grow all the Mediterranean herbs plus mints, borage, summer savory, horseradish, and more. Putting supper together begins with a perusal of the garden to see which herbs are at their best; the other ingredients come next.

Almost all of the herbs listed in this book will flower, sprinkling your herb garden with pretty blossoms. Mix and match, contrast and compare—you can make dramatic and attractive arrangements in dedicated herb gardens, dot herbs through beds and borders, or simply keep a few pots outside the backdoor. This regenerating store cupboard of flavors will ensure triumphant, tasty meals.

*Jeff Cox*

## A NOTE FROM THE COOK MARIE-PIERRE MOINE

As a cook, herbs are my best friends. Just a handful brightens up my emergency store cupboard concoctions: dried pasta and canned tomatoes cry out for warming, peppery basil; green beans and flaked tuna for robust parsley and gentle chives; and rice and frozen peas for scented thyme or sage. Half a clove of crushed garlic will not go amiss in any of these impromptu scenarios either.

When I am preparing a more gourmet, formal meal, herbs are wonderful allies, too. And they have power in numbers, so I love putting together a palette of mixed herbs—a bed of rosemary sprigs and thyme underneath a shoulder of lamb, a generous scattering of dried fennel and mustard seeds over belly of pork, and tarragon and parsley in a buttery pan of fried tomatoes. At the end of cooking, I add a scattering of fresh herbs to give a flourish of visual appeal and palate-tingling top notes.

As an urban dweller, I am unable to have a proper herb garden but every year I manage a couple of pots on the windowsill and have never found the need to buy herbs—in the growing months, at least.

Running a hand through stems of rosemary or pinching off basil leaves lifts the spirits, but don't despair if you cannot have fresh herbs permanently on tap; remember that many freeze well. When freezer space is at a premium, herbs should be a priority—a ginger root, a roll of herb butter, or a cilantro ice cube are all well worth their shelf space.

# CHOOSE

With a huge variety of herbs available,
you need to know what flavors you want,
how you can use them, and where and
how to grow the plants. Whether in a
window box, a pot, or in the garden,
there's an herb here for everyone.

## PLANTED POTS AND BASKETS

The culinary-themed window boxes show you how to
produce a whole store cupboard of flavors in one pot.
These are just a guide, and you can mix and match
them to suit your needs and personal tastes.

KEY:

FROST HARDINESS
❄ Half-hardy
❄❄ Frost-hardy
❄❄❄ Hardy

GROWING CONDITIONS
☼ Prefers sun
◐ Prefers partial shade
● Prefers shade
💧 Tolerant of wet soil

DIMENSIONS
↕ Height  ↔ Spread

# EVERYDAY ESSENTIALS

There are some herbs that you return to time and time again to invigorate your cooking. You can make ordinary everyday meals extraordinary with just a handful of these herbs: perk up a roast chicken with sage, add depth to a tomato salad with basil leaves, enliven pasta sauce with oregano, or make a salsa with cilantro leaves. And, of course, no cook should be without a fresh supply of thyme and parsley.

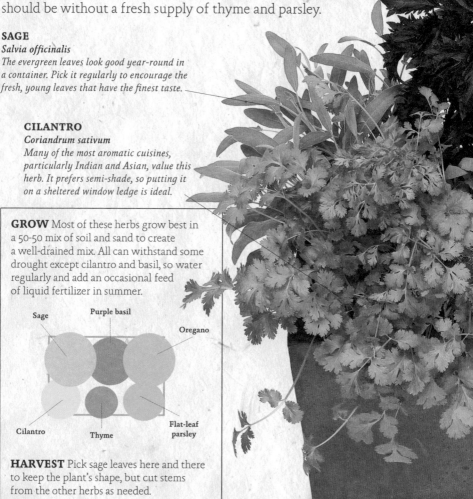

**SAGE**
*Salvia officinalis*
*The evergreen leaves look good year-round in a container. Pick it regularly to encourage the fresh, young leaves that have the finest taste.*

**CILANTRO**
*Coriandrum sativum*
*Many of the most aromatic cuisines, particularly Indian and Asian, value this herb. It prefers semi-shade, so putting it on a sheltered window ledge is ideal.*

**GROW** Most of these herbs grow best in a 50-50 mix of soil and sand to create a well-drained mix. All can withstand some drought except cilantro and basil, so water regularly and add an occasional feed of liquid fertilizer in summer.

Sage    Purple basil    Oregano

Cilantro    Thyme    Flat-leaf parsley

**HARVEST** Pick sage leaves here and there to keep the plant's shape, but cut stems from the other herbs as needed.

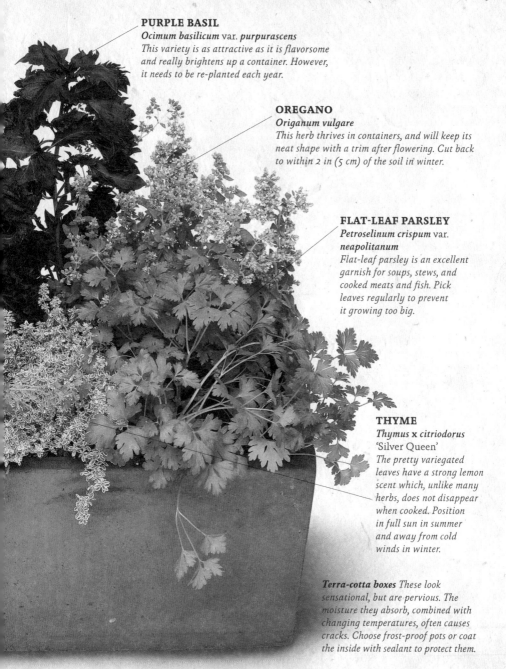

**PURPLE BASIL**
*Ocimum basilicum* var. *purpurascens*
This variety is as attractive as it is flavorsome
and really brightens up a container. However,
it needs to be re-planted each year.

**OREGANO**
*Origanum vulgare*
This herb thrives in containers, and will keep its
neat shape with a trim after flowering. Cut back
to within 2 in (5 cm) of the soil in winter.

**FLAT-LEAF PARSLEY**
*Petroselinum crispum* var.
*neapolitanum*
Flat-leaf parsley is an excellent
garnish for soups, stews, and
cooked meats and fish. Pick
leaves regularly to prevent
it growing too big.

**THYME**
*Thymus* x *citriodorus*
'Silver Queen'
The pretty variegated
leaves have a strong lemon
scent which, unlike many
herbs, does not disappear
when cooked. Position
in full sun in summer
and away from cold
winds in winter.

*Terra-cotta boxes* These look
sensational, but are pervious. The
moisture they absorb, combined with
changing temperatures, often causes
cracks. Choose frost-proof pots or coat
the inside with sealant to protect them.

# SALAD HERBS

Each of these herbs has a distinctive flavor, so they should be used in salads in small amounts—except chervil, where more is better. They will happily grow side by side, and can also be used together in recipes, except dill, whose warm caraway-like flavor tends to dominate. Tarragon is a perennial, but the others are annuals or biennials and so will need replacing every year or two.

**DILL**
*Anethum graveolens*
*Put in its final position when planting this box, as dill doesn't like to be moved. It pairs well with seafood, making an excellent marinade.*

**ARUGULA**
*Eruca vesicaria* subsp. *sativa*
*The young leaves have a mild, peppery, pungent flavor, which becomes more pronounced with age. Pick leaves regularly to encourage fresh growth.*

**GROW** These herbs prefer a rich, well-drained, moist (but not wet) soil. Use a 50–50 mix of good garden soil and compost and water regularly, particularly in hot temperatures.

Dill      French tarragon      Chives

Arugula      Curly parsley      Chervil

Pinch off the tips of the herbs to get leaves with full flavor, but allow dill to flower if you are growing it for its seeds.

**HARVEST** Pick arugula's outer individual leaves but the whole stems of the others.

## FRENCH TARRAGON
**Artemisia dracunculus French**
*Plant French not Russian tarragon if you want the licorice flavor. Use young plants or grow from cuttings. It is a strong-flavored herb, so use it sparingly.*

## CHIVES
**Allium schoenoprasum**
*Chives add a delicate onion aroma and flavor to salads and salsas. Cut individual stems 1 in (2.5 cm) above soil level and use snipped into small pieces.*

## CHERVIL
**Anthriscus cerefolium**
*The sweetest herb, in all respects. Chervil's dainty leaves have a licorice and parsley flavor. Plant it in a semi-shady position if you can, as sun causes it to flower too quickly.*

## CURLY PARSLEY
**Petroselinum crispum**
*This neat herb is perfect for growing in containers; it looks pretty and will not take over the space. Chop the leaves finely and sprinkle over salads.*

***Wooden container*** *Drill holes in the base of the container to allow excess moisture to drain away. Line the container with black plastic before adding soil, to preserve the wood, and puncture holes in the lining to correspond with those in the base.*

# MEDITERRANEAN POTS

These herbs are native to the Mediterranean regions. They thrive in free-draining soil and produce the greatest abundance of fragrant, volatile oils when positioned in full sun in hot, dry summers. Mediterranean cuisine is famed for its fresh tastes, and much of that reputation comes from these herbs.

**SWEET BASIL**
*Ocimum basilicum* 'Genovese'
*Being an annual Mediterranean herb, basil needs sowing under cover each spring, or can be grown indoors on a sunny windowsill.*

**THYME**
*Thymus vulgaris*
*The most well-known variety of this evergreen perennial; it is used in poultry, pork, and fish dishes and in bouquets garnis (see p128).*

**ROSEMARY**
*Rosmarinus officinalis*
*This evergreen perennial form has a strong, piney scent and flavor. It needs regular trimming to keep it in check.*

**GROW** Use free-draining soil, add extra grit to compost if necessary. Plant herbs mixing textures and colors and ensure the pots have some winter use by planting a perennial with each annual.

Sweet basil · Rosemary · Thyme

English lavender · Sweet basil · Purple sage · Sweet basil · Thyme

Greek oregano · Purple basil · Thyme

Water if the leaves droop. Pinch out the tips of the basil and oregano for more leafy growth.

**HARVEST** Pick basil leaves individually, trim sage leaves here and there to maintain shape.

**ENGLISH LAVENDER**
*Lavandula angustifolia*
Use the flowers and evergreen
leaves of this perennial
sparingly in syrups and sugars.

**SWEET BASIL**
*Ocimum basilicum*
'Green Ruffles'
and 'Napolitano'
These annual basils have
a spicy licorice taste.

**GREEK OREGANO**
*Origanum vulgare* subsp. *hirtum* 'Greek'
This hardy perennial species has dark,
aromatic leaves. It is popular in
Greek and Turkish dishes.

**PURPLE SAGE**
*Salvia officinalis*
'Purpurascens'
The leaves of this
evergreen perennial
can be picked all year.

**PURPLE BASIL**
*Ocimum basilicum* var. *purpurascens*
This variety has strongly scented
and richly colorful leaves.

**Terra-cotta pots** *These
develop a fine patina
over time. The whitish
salt build-up adds
character to them.*

# MIDDLE EASTERN

Classic dishes from Turkey to Morocco owe their rich, deep flavors to the herb-garden favorites that feature in this zinc container. Traditionally these dishes are accompanied by hot mint tea, which is why this blend of herbs also contains spearmint and another favorite for tea, anise hyssop.

### CILANTRO
***Coriandrum sativum***
*As a warmth-loving herb, cilantro thrives in pots that can be moved to sunny spots. Trim regularly to encourage leaves, or leave it alone if you want seeds.*

**GROW** All these herbs like well-drained, good-quality potting soil, so add extra grit if necessary. Let cilantro flower if you want its seeds. Pinch the growing tip of anise hyssop when young for tender leafy shoots. Water when the soil begins to dry out.

Anise hyssop

Spearmint

Cilantro

Thyme

Flat-leaf parsley

**HARVEST** Select individual stems or side branches, or take leaves from here and there.

**ANISE HYSSOP**
*Agastache foeniculum*
This herb has a distinct licorice flavor in its pretty leaves. It needs protection in hard frosts.

**SPEARMINT**
*Mentha spicata*
Spearmint is the most widely grown of all mints. It makes refreshing teas and, in the Middle East, is a key ingredient in tabbouleh (see p152).

**FLAT-LEAF PARSLEY**
*Petroselinum crispum*
var. *neapolitanum*
To ensure a constant supply, sow seed in pots at regular intervals from spring and transfer to the main pot as necessary.

**THYME**
*Thymus vulgaris*
The piney, resinous aroma and flavor of thyme is an essential ingredient in Middle Eastern cooking. It is used in lamb tagines and many other dishes.

**Zinc container** Make a few holes to let excess water drain out and put stones in the base of the pot to aid drainage. Only the mint can tolerate wet roots.

# HARDY HERBS

With the exception of rosemary, which needs a winter mulch in some areas, these herbs will survive temperatures down to -20°F (-29°C) and return in spring. Provide enough room for their roots, as they can grow for years.

**GREEK OREGANO**
*Origanum vulgare* subsp. *hirtum* 'Greek'
*A more intense version of common oregano, with round, dark green, resinous, peppery leaves.*

**ORANGE-SCENTED THYME**
*Thymus* x *citriodorus* 'Fragrantissimus'
*This variety has evergreen variegated leaves with a distinct citrussy scent. Pick the leaves year-round.*

**GROW** Plant in decent well-drained garden soil with added compost. Remove the top 2 in (5 cm) of soil in spring and replace with fresh compost.

Greek oregano

Roman chamomile

Rosemary

Sorrel

Orange-scented thyme

Sage

Winter savory

**HARVEST** Cut stems or individual leaves for sorrel and pick chamomile's flowers just as they form buds.

**ROMAN CHAMOMILE**
*Chamaemelum nobile*
This is the hardy perennial variety, rather than the German annual. Use the flower buds in teas, or let them open to create a pretty feature here.

**SORREL**
*Rumex acetosa*
Sorrel is a tangy, sharply acidic, leafy plant. Remove any flower heads as they appear to keep fresh, new leaves coming.

**ROSEMARY**
*Rosmarinus officinalis*
The resinous quality of this herb recalls pine and camphor. It is good with potatoes, lamb, and in oils.

**WINTER SAVORY**
*Satureja montana*
This semi-evergreen perennial needs winter protection. Use this potent herb in small amounts.

**SAGE**
*Salvia officinalis*
The leaves can be used in sauces (see p164), with poultry (see p139), or in butter for pasta, Italian-style. They can also be used fresh to make a soothing tea.

*Wooden crate* This is roomy enough for these vigorous herbs, but if they get too big, lift and divide them when growth is slow, in fall or early spring (see p91). Pot on the new extra plants and return one to the crate.

# HERBAL TEAS

The most elegant and flavorsome teas are made using fresh herbs, as the fine fragrance and flavor compounds in their leaves evaporate and disintegrate soon after they're picked. This group includes herbs that can be used to make teas to suit all palates and moods.

**LEMON BALM**
*Melissa officinalis*
*Use young leaves for a mild lemon-and-mint flavor. Self-sows readily, so root out unwanted seedlings.*

**BERGAMOT**
*Monarda didyma*
*Bergamot makes an excellent herb tea. Dig up plants every three years and divide them.*

**SWEET WOODRUFF**
*Galium odoratum*
*Use sparingly—you need only a stem or two for a mild, vanilla-flavored tea. Plant under the other herbs, as it likes some shade.*

**GROW** Use potting mix or well-drained garden soil. These plants like moist soil, so tuck dried grass clippings around the base of the stems to conserve moisture. Pinch back the lemon verbena and trim the fennel.

**HARVEST** Cut just a couple of stems of sweet woodruff and take leaves here and there from the other herbs.

Lemon balm
Bronze fennel
Lemon verbena
Bergamot
Moroccan mint
Sweet woodruff
German chamomile
Sweet marjoram

**BRONZE FENNEL**
*Foeniculum vulgare* 'Purpureum'
*With its licorice flavor, this fennel makes*
*a mild tea. Trim the tops for leafy growth.*

**LEMON VERBENA**
*Aloysia triphylla*
*With its fragrance and flavor of*
*lemon but without the acid zing, lemon*
*verbena is ideal for tea. Cut back*
*stems once the leaves have dropped.*

**MOROCCAN MINT**
*Mentha spicata* **var.**
*crispa* 'Moroccan'
*This variety has a fresh*
*spearmint flavor. It is*
*widely drunk as a tea in*
*North Africa. Sink it into*
*the box in a small pot to*
*control its growth.*

**SWEET MARJORAM**
*Origanum majorana*
*Sweet marjoram is less assertive*
*than oregano and so makes a*
*sweet, lightly spicy tea with*
*a mild camphor note. An annual,*
*it needs re-sowing each year.*

**GERMAN CHAMOMILE**
*Matricaria recutita*
*This annual chamomile is much preferred*
*for tea over the perennial Roman*
*chamomile, which has a bitter taste.*
*Again, it needs re-sowing each year.*

***Wicker basket*** *Weaved wicker gives this*
*arrangement a rustic feel. Position it in a sunny*
*spot in summer and move it to a sheltered position*
*as the plants die back in fall and winter.*

# THE HERB CATALOG

What is an herb? A plant needs certain qualities to be an herb; here you will find plants that can simply be used to add flavor to your cooking and can be grown in temperate climates. In different cuisines these plants are used in a variety of ways. The leaves, flowers, seeds, or roots are often edible; in some cases leaves and stems are used as "pot herbs", meaning they are boiled and served as a vegetable.

## ONION
### *Allium* spp.

These members of the large onion family are useful culinary herbs as well as kitchen staples. They are drought-resistant, and, because they are onions, they rarely have pest problems.

**GROW** For all these allium species, sweeten good garden soil with wood ash or ground limestone before planting sets or sowing seed, for best results. Ideally, plant garlic in fall, but you can also plant it in spring along with onions and chives.

**HARVEST** Dig up bulbils in summer to use or store (see p118) and pick leaves and flowers throughout the growing season as they are needed.

**COOK** Both garlic and onion bulbils can be used in a wide range of savory dishes as a flavoring. They keep their flavor well when cooked. Leaves of all the allium species are best used raw.

*Green-stemmed garlic is known as green garlic. It is not fully mature and so has a milder taste*

### ▲ CHIVES
*Allium schoenoprasum*
❀ ❀ ❀ ☼
The bulbs multiply in good soil, so grow chives in a pot to control them. Pick leaves and flowers a few at a time as needed.
**HABIT** Slim hollow stalks
↕ 12 in (30 cm)
↔ 18 in (45 cm)
**COOK'S NOTES** Use leaves and flowers whole or snipped as a garnish or to flavor eggs, salads, and soured cream.

### GARLIC ▶
*Allium sativum*
❀ ❀ ❀ ☼
Plant bulbils in good soil in full sun in fall. Dig up the heads when the tops are dry.
**HABIT** Hollow stalks
↕ 18 in (45 cm)
↔ 9–12 in (23–30 cm)
**COOK'S NOTES** Add to sauces, stews, butters, oils, and many other dishes.

### ◄ ROCAMBOLE
*Allium sativum* var. *ophioscorodon*
❀❀❀ ☀

Plant bulbils in fall in good garden soil. Cut the leaves in spring, dig up the purple and white bulbils in the fall. It has a mild garlic flavor.
**HABIT** Hollow stalks
↕ 18 in (45 cm) ↔ 9–12 in (23–30 cm)
**COOK'S NOTES** Use the leaves as you would chives and the bulbils as you would garlic.

*The broad leaves have a strong garlicky aroma*

### WILD GARLIC ►
*Allium ursinum*
❀❀❀ ☀ ☀

Sow this perennial direct into the garden in moist soil in semi-shade or shade in fall. Divide established plants in late summer. All parts can be eaten; pick leaves and flowers as needed, bulbils in fall.
**HABIT** Hollow stalks
↕ 14–18 in (36–45 cm) ↔ 12 in (30 cm)
**COOK'S NOTES** Add leaves and flowers to salads, or to garnish potato or egg dishes. Use bulbils in soups, cream sauces, and in risotto.

*Young leaves have a sweeter garlic flavor*

### GARLIC CHIVES ►
*Allium tuberosum*
❀❀❀ ☀

Plant in spring in good soil. Divide clumps every three years. Cut a few stems as needed.
**HABIT** Flat-bladed stalks
↕ 12 in (30 cm)
↔ 6–8 in (15–20 cm)
**COOK'S NOTES** Add to potato salads.

*The leaves of green onion are round and hollow*

### GREEN ONION ►
*Allium fistulosum*
❀❀❀ ☀

Plant sets or sow seed in spring. Divide clumps every 3 years in spring. Harvest the oniony bulbs 5–6 weeks after planting.
**HABIT** Hollow stalks
↕ 8–10 in (20–25 cm) ↔ 6 in (15 cm)
**COOK'S NOTES** Use in egg dishes, quiches, and savory tarts.

# ANISE HYSSOP
### *Agastache foeniculum*

This relative of mint has minty, licorice-flavored leaves and flowers. It is a perennial, and bees love its pretty purple flower spikes in summer.

*The small top leaves make the finest tea*

✳✳☼☀

**GROW** Take cuttings or divide plants in spring, or start seed indoors in late winter. Plant out seedlings into good garden soil when all risk of frost has passed. This plant is happiest in full sun and rich, moist soil, but tolerates partial shade.
**HARVEST** The leaves have the best flavor just before the plant flowers.
**COOK** Add the leaves and flowers to salads for a mild minty licorice flavor, or brew them as a tea.

**HABIT** Upright, leafy
↕ 24–36 in (60–90 cm) ↔ 18 in (45 cm)

# LEMON VERBENA
### *Aloysia triphylla*

The leaves of perennial lemon verbena grow vigorously on long stems, but they keep their lemony scent to themselves until disturbed.

✳✳☼

**GROW** Plant cuttings in the garden, after all danger of frost has passed, into well-drained, dry soil in full sun. A tender herb, it is best to plant it in a large pot sunk into the ground so it can be moved indoors in fall in cold regions. In warmer, frost-free areas you can leave it outside over winter.
**HARVEST** Leaves can be harvested here and there from the plant and used fresh.
**COOK** Brew the leaves for citrussy tisanes, use them to make lemony vinegars and oils, or finely chop them and add to salads and fruit desserts.

**HABIT** Upright, bushy
↕ 10 ft (3 m) ↔ 10 ft (3 m))

# AMARANTH
### *Amaranthus hypochondriacus*

This annual is a global favorite, with spinach-flavored leaves and seeds that contain 30 percent more high-lysine protein than most cereals.

❀ ☼

**GROW** Sow seed directly into the garden each spring. This herb grows in full sun in almost any kind of soil. Grain amaranth can yield up to 2.2 lb (1 kg) of grain per plant, so you may need to stake the plants to support their seedheads.

**HARVEST** Pick leaves as needed, and cut the seedheads with their stems for drying and to collect their seeds (see p116).

**COOK** Add young leaves to salads and cook mature leaves as you would spinach. Cook seeds in a little water, or in a dry pan to eat as "popcorn".

**HABIT** Upright, bushy
↕ 4–5 ft (1.2–1.5 m) ↔ 18–24 in (45–60 cm)

*Seeds can be cooked with three parts water to make a "porridge"*

# DILL
### *Anethum graveolens*

The umbrella-shaped seedheads of this annual bear seeds that are popular for pickling, and the feathery leaves are an excellent flavoring.

❀ ❀ ❀ ☼

**GROW** Dill is easy to grow from seed; sow in mid-spring in a sunny spot in good, well-drained garden soil where you want it to grow, as it resents disturbance. Position it near plants that will benefit from the insects it attracts. Make successive sowings throughout the summer to keep the crop coming.

**HARVEST** Use the leaves fresh or dried. Let the seed ripen on the plant before harvesting it (see p106).

**COOK** Use the seeds in vinegars and teas. Use fresh or dried fronds with salads, and soups; dill goes well with fish, especially salmon, and is a key ingredient in gravlax.

**HABIT** Upright hollow stems
↕ 24–36 in (60–90 cm) ↔ 6–12 in (15–30 cm)

# ANGELICA
*Angelica archangelica*

The leaves and stems of this pretty biennial have an aroma of juniper berries, hence its use in making gin. The seeds and root are edible too.

❋❋❋☼

**GROW** Sow seed in fall or spring in semi-shade in a moist, compost-enriched soil where you want it to grow, as its long tap root (the main, largest, vertical root) will not transplant. Water it well in summer, as it dislikes hot, dry conditions. Allow it to set seed in late summer if you want to collect seed or let it self-seed. It will die after setting seed.

**HARVEST** Take leaves here and there or cut off side shoots before the plant flowers. Collect seeds as they ripen (see p106). Harvest and dry roots in the second fall just after flowering.

**COOK** Seeds add a touch of sweetness to drinks; use leaves in custards, marmalades, fruit desserts, and teas; or make candied angelica to decorate cakes.

**HABIT** Upright, leafy
↕ 12–24 in (30–60 cm) ↔ 9–12 in (23–30 cm)

# CHERVIL
*Anthriscus cerefolium*

This annual herb is one of the culinary *fines herbes*, along with chives, parsley, and tarragon. Its lacy leaves have a light licorice flavor.

❋❋❋☼

**GROW** Sow seed in moist, compost-enriched soil in a cool, semi-shady spot each spring as temperatures begin to rise. Sow where you want it to grow, as it has a large tap root and dislikes being transplanted. Keep an eye on this plant in summer, as it quickly runs to seed in hot, sunny conditions.

**HARVEST** Pick leaves from here and there over the plant. Chervil loses flavor when dried, so use the leaves fresh.

**COOK** The subtle licorice flavor is fragile, so add the leaves fresh at the last minute to salads and to finish creamy poultry dishes.

**HABIT** Upright, leafy
↕ 10 ft (3 m) ↔ 10 ft (3 m)

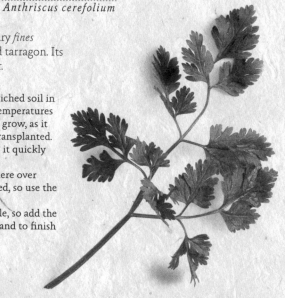

# SMALLAGE
### *Apium graveolens*

The seeds and leaves of this biennial, wild form of celery have a more intense celery flavor and aroma than the related, large, modern stalks.

✤✤✤◐☼

**GROW** Sow seed in early spring under cover. Plant out seedlings in full sun in rich soil in the bottom of a shallow trench in the garden, when all risk of frost has passed. Keep the soil well-watered in summer. Let the plant produce its flower heads and set seed if you want to harvest the seeds.

**HARVEST** Cut individual stalks or the whole plant as and when needed. Harvest the seeds when they are ripe and falling from the seedheads (see p106).

**COOK** Use fresh leaves in salads and sauces, and add the seeds to stews and casseroles.

**HABIT** Tall, slender stems
↕ 1–3 ft (30 cm–1 m) ↔ 6–12 in (15–30 cm)

*The leaves resemble those of its cousin, parsley*

# HORSERADISH
### *Armoracia rusticana*

Originally considered a medicinal herb, this perennial is now grown as a culinary herb for its strongly flavored large tap root and leaves.

✤✤✤☼

**GROW** Horseradish can be invasive, so plant cuttings or divisions in a large pot sunk into the soil. You need space; the large, wavy-edged leaves spread 2–3 ft² (60–90 cm²). Choose a sunny spot in sandy, well-drained loam. Enrich with compost in fall and late spring.

**HARVEST** Dig up the plant to take pieces of root as needed—the herb is most pungent when freshly dug. Harvest and store all roots in fall (see p107).

**COOK** The freshly grated root works wonders mixed with cream to make a sauce, and served with beef or smoked fish.

**HABIT** Upright, clump-forming
↕ 1–4 ft (30 cm–1.2 m) ↔ 24–36 in (60–90 cm)

*Young leaves can be added to salads*

*The real flavor is in the root*

# FRENCH TARRAGON
*Artemisia dracunculus* French

The flavor of perennial French tarragon is much superior to that of the Russian variety, so cooks prefer to use its licorice-flavored leaves.

❀❀❀☼

**GROW** This herb doesn't set viable seed, so it must be propagated by root cuttings taken after the first frosts are over (see p90). Plant them out in a warm, dry, sunny spot. Renew old plants by dividing clumps in spring.

**HARVEST** Pick sprigs of leaves when needed to use fresh. Tarragon freezes well but loses much of its flavor when dried.

**COOK** Use fresh in omelets, salads, chicken dishes, and in cream sauces, or to flavor white wine vinegar (see p135).

**HABIT** Upright, leafy
↕ 18–36 in (45 cm–1 m) ↔ 12–15 in (30–38 cm)

# BORAGE
*Borago officinalis*

An herb-garden favorite, this annual is cherished more for its sky-blue petals than its leaves, both of which have a cucumber flavor.

❀❀❀☼

**GROW** Sow seed directly in the garden in mid-spring in well-drained, light soil in a sunny spot. Keep the soil moist during the growing season.

**HARVEST** Cut young stems for fresh leaves throughout the summer, and pick flowers to use fresh, or to freeze or dry.

**COOK** Chop the fresh leaves to add to yogurt, cream, and cucumber salads. Use flowers in drinks such as Pimm's, in ice cubes, salads, or candied to decorate cakes.

**HABIT** Upright, branching
↕ 1–3 ft (30 cm–1 m) ↔ 6–12 in (15–30 cm)

*The hairs on young leaves dissolve in the mouth on eating*

# MUSTARDS

*Brassica* spp.

Grow these annual plants for their peppery leaves and for their seeds, which are used to make the familiar condiment. Black mustard is the most pungent, India is the bitterest.

❀ ❀ ❀ ☼

**GROW** Sow seed in fall in soil enriched with well-rotted manure or compost. The seedlings will emerge in the spring. Alternatively, sow in spring once all risk of frost has passed. Each seed makes a single stem with many flowers, so sow thickly to allow the stems to support one another.

**HARVEST** Cut the stems with their seed pods just before the seeds ripen and let them dry (see p116). Pick young leaves and flowers all summer.

**COOK** Add both the leaves and flowers to salads and stir-fry dishes. Crush the seeds for homemade mustard, or add to salad dressings or sauces.

*The young seed pods can be pickled*

### ◀ INDIA MUSTARD

*Brassica juncea*

The crinkled-edged leaves have a warm peppery flavor and look pretty in the garden. The seeds are slightly bitter and are less potent than the black ones.

**HABIT** Upright, clump-forming
↕ 3–4 ft (1–1.2 m) ↔ 12 in (30 cm)

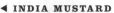

*The flowers are also edible, with a mild mustard flavor*

### BLACK MUSTARD ▶

*Brassica nigra*

Black mustard is harder to find than India, so it is worth growing your own. The leaves and seeds have a strong flavor and heat.

**HABIT** Upright, clump-forming
↕ 3–4 ft (1–1.2 m) ↔ 12 in (30 cm)

# CALAMINT
### *Calamintha* sp.

It is strange that this pretty perennial herb isn't better known for its pleasant minty, peppery, but slightly bitter leaves and flowers.

✿✿✿☼☽

**GROW** Start cuttings in pots in early spring, or sow directly into well-drained soil once it has warmed up. Or divide plants in spring. It prefers a slightly alkaline soil, so sweeten acid soil with wood ash or ground limestone. New growth needs protection from severe frosts.

**HARVEST** Pick leaves when the plant is not in flower for the best flavor. Harvest flowers as and when needed.

**COOK** Use to flavor drinks, finely chop very young leaves and use in salads. Lesser calamint (*Calamintha nepeta*) has the strongest potency, so use it sparingly.

**HABIT** Low-growing, bushy
↕ 18 in (45 cm) ↔ 20–30 in (50–75 cm)

*All parts of the plant have a delicious aroma of mint*

# POT MARIGOLD
### *Calendula officinalis*

This annual was once known as poor man's saffron because the sweet, edible, yellow or orange flowers are used to dye foods.

*Pick the flowers regularly to encourage more blooms*

✿✿✿☼☽

**GROW** Sow seed in pots indoors in fall or in well-drained soil in full sun or partial shade after the last frosts in spring. Transplant into pots or good garden soil in late spring. Marigold is hardy and will overwinter outside in warm climates. The plant produces a small bunch of leaves from which tall daisy-like flowers rise. If growing it in the garden, thin out plants to keep them 12–18 in (30–45 cm) apart.

**HARVEST** Pick flowers regularly when they are young and fresh.

**COOK** You can use the aromatic, slightly bitter petals to decorate salads, or add them to fish and meat stews.

**HABIT** Bushy, leafy
↕ 20–28 in (50–70 cm) ↔ 20–28 in (50–70 cm)

# CHILE PEPPERS

*Capsicum* spp.

There are hundreds of chile pepper varieties available, but listed here are a few of the most popular ones. The plants are perennials in the tropics and annuals in temperate zones.

❀ ☼

**GROW** Sow seed in pots and plant out young plants in rich soil in a sunny position when risk of frost has passed. Mulch the plants and keep the mulch moist to recreate the hot, humid conditions they like.

**HARVEST** Pepper fruits can range from pea-sized to large cylinders or blocky types. Young peppers are green but ripen to red, yellow, orange, chocolate brown, and other colors. Cut the stems of fruits with scissors when harvesting.

**COOK** Handle them carefully, scrape out the seeds to lessen their heat, or leave them in for a hotter sensation and the inimitable chile pepper flavor (see p126). They can be used fresh, dried, in flakes, or ground to spice up many recipes.

### ◀ SERRANO
*Capsicum annuum*
The green peppers ripen to red and have very hot, pungent seeds.
**HABIT** Bushy
↕ Varies, mostly 2–4 ft (60 cm–1.2 m)
↔ 20–36 in (50–90 cm)
**COOK'S NOTES** Use in sauces.

## BIRD PEPPER ▶
*Capsicum annuum*
These tiny peppers can be red, orange, or green; their size is deceptive, as they are very, very hot.
**HABIT** Bushy
↕ Varies, mostly 2–4 ft (60 cm–1.2 m)
↔ 20–36 in (50–90 cm)
**COOK'S NOTES** Use whole to add heat to curries.

## JALAPEÑO ▶
*Capsicum annuum*
A commonly used pepper; when green they are medium-hot, and when ripe and red they are less hot and sweeter.
**HABIT** Bushy
↕ Varies, mostly 2–4 ft (60 cm–1.2 m)
↔ 20–36 in (50–90cm)
**COOK'S NOTES** Pickle or use as a condiment.

### SCOTCH BONNET ▶
*Capsicum chinense*
These are one of the hottest peppers on earth. They start yellow-green and ripen to orange-red.
**HABIT** Bushy
↕ Varies, mostly 2–4 ft (60 cm–1.2 m)
↔ 20–36 in (50–90 cm)
**COOK'S NOTES** Use to flavor Caribbean sauces.

*Scotch Bonnet's lantern-shaped fruits are incredibly hot*

# CAPER BUSH
### *Capparis spinosa*

Although a tender native of Mediterranean climates, this evergreen shrub will tolerate warm winters elsewhere, and produces tasty buds.

✹ ✹ ☼

**GROW** Sow seed indoors in early spring or take cuttings. Plant out when risk of frost has passed. It needs good drainage and dry soil. Flower buds are borne on new stems each year, so cut back plants each fall. Plants raised from seed will not flower for four or five years.
**HARVEST** Pick flower buds for pickling before they open.
**COOK** Use the salted or pickled buds in oil- or butter-based sauces, and dressings with fish and cold meats.

**HABIT** Shrubby
↕ 3 ft (1 m) ↔ 5 ft (1.5 m)

*Caper bush's pretty white flowers are very ornamental*

# CARAWAY
### *Carum carvi*

The leaves and seeds of this aromatic, parsley-chervil flavored biennial are often considered spices, but the root can be used as a pot herb.

✹ ✹ ✹ ☼

**GROW** Sow seed outdoors in mid-spring in good, well-drained soil in full sun. Once established caraway needs no supplementary feeding, but keep it free of competition from weeds.
**HARVEST** Gather young leaves as and when required. Cut stems for drying when the seed begins to separate easily from the plant. Dig up plants for the roots in the fall of their second year.
**COOK** Use young leaves in salads or soups. Add the seeds to cakes, breads, cookies, cabbage, cheese dishes, and meat stews.

**HABIT** Upright, bushy
↕ 3 ft (1 m) ↔ 12–15 in (30–38 cm)

*Young leaves are less pungent than the seeds*

# CHAMOMILE

*Chamaemelum nobile* and *Matricaria recutita*

Perennial Roman chamomile makes a pretty lawn and releases a warm apple scent when walked over. The leaves of annual German chamomile are used to make a soothing tea.

✿ ✿ ✿ ☼

**GROW** Sow seeds of Roman and German chamomiles under cover in spring. Plant out in well-drained, sandy soil in full sun when all risk of frost has passed. For a lawn, plant close together and cut regularly to encourage dense growth.
**HARVEST** Cut leaves in spring and early summer; pick flowers when fully open, in midsummer.
**COOK** Use the flowers and leaves fresh or dried to make tea; the leaves make a milder brew.

*The conical centers of the flowers are dried to use in making tea*

**▲ ROMAN CHAMOMILE**
*Chamaemelum nobile*
The perennial chamomile has sweet, aromatic, evergreen, lacy foliage with tiny daisy-like flowers. Clip the flowers in the first year and weed around the plant often.
**HABIT** Low-growing, mat-forming
↕ 6–9 in (15–22 cm)
↔ indefinite

**GERMAN CHAMOMILE ▶**
*Matricaria recutita*
Plant out seedlings of this annual, flowery flavored chamomile when they have no more than three true leaves, as they then resent transplanting. Self-sows readily.
**HABIT** Upright, branching leaves
↕ 24–30 in (60–75 cm) ↔ 2 ft (60 cm)

# GOOD KING HENRY/FAT HEN

*Chenopodium* spp.

The leaves of Good King Henry have a licorice flavor while those of Fat Hen have a spinach-like taste. Both are very nutritious, being rich in iron, calcium, and vitamins B1 and C.

❀ ❀ ☼

**GROW** Easily grown in spring from seed sown in well-drained freshly dug soil, or from divisions. These plants are tough survivors and take care of themselves. They like full sun and may need water during droughts.

**HARVEST** Cut young stems to use like asparagus. Pick young leaves as needed, or harvest larger leaves in summer for cooking.

**COOK** Use both varieties as a pot herb or eat the young leaves raw in salads.

### GOOD KING HENRY

*Chenopodium bonus-henricus*
This perennial herb resents transplanting, but grows like a weed when established, so you will need to control it.
**HABIT** Upright, leafy
↕ 24–36 in (60–90 cm) ↔ 12–18 in (30–45 cm)
**COOK'S NOTES** It has an assertive flavor, so use its slightly bitter, lemony leaves sparingly either fresh or dried when cooking beans and pulses.

### FAT HEN

*Chenopodium album*
As a fast-growing annual, Fat Hen will sow itself at will. Remove seedlings if you want to keep it under control.
**HABIT** Upright, leafy
↕ 1–6 ft (30 cm–1.8 m)
↔ 18–24 in (45–60 cm)
**COOK'S NOTES** Use the leaves in mixed green vegetable dishes or in soups; chop finely to add sparingly to salads.

*Wash leaves carefully to remove any grit*

*The leaves are shaped like the imprint of a goose foot*

# CHICORY
## *Cichorium intybus*

There are many types of this herb, and their leaves, stems, and flowers are used in cuisines around the world.

❀ ❀ ❀ ☼

**GROW** Sow seed directly into the garden in mid-spring. Cultivated varieties like rich, deep, and well-drained soil to make large tap roots. Give the plants a mid-summer dressing of rich compost. Keep the soil moist but not wet.

**HARVEST** Cut leaves for salads when very young to use fresh, as older plants develop a bitter, milky sap. Pick flowers in early summer to use fresh or to dry. Dig up roots throughout the summer, or in fall.

**COOK** Add young leaves and flowers to salads; lift young roots and boil and serve with a white sauce.

*The bitter taste of the leaves mellows when grilled or roasted*

**RADICCHIO ▶**
*Cichorium intybus*
Cut the bitter, colorful leaves of this annual here and there in mid-summer, then let the plant grow on undisturbed to produce tight heads for fall.
**HABIT** Upright, tight head of leaves
↕ 6–8 in (15–20 cm) ↔ 8–10 in (20–25 cm)
**COOK'S NOTES** Add the leaves to salads, chargrill with olive oil, or roast, or stew.

**BELGIAN ENDIVE ▶**
*Cichorium intybus*
Keep the tall leaves of this perennial pale for a less bitter flavor. Pot up the plants in early winter and put them in a dark place indoors for 4–6 weeks to "force" chicons, which are blanched stems.
**HABIT** Upright, tight head of leaves
↕ 24 in (60 cm) ↔ 12 in (30 cm)
**COOK'S NOTES** Use leaves in winter salads with walnuts and a creamy dressing, sprinkle chicons with lemon juice and steam, or bake with cheese and ham.

**▲ LOOSELEAF CHICORY**
*Cichorium intybus* 'Roseum'
Sow seed of this mild-tasting annual in spring for a winter crop. This variety has pink flowers, but most have blue flowers.
**HABIT** Upright
↕ 18–24 in (45–60 cm) ↔ 8–10 in (20–25 cm)
**COOK'S NOTES** Dry roots, then roast and grind them to use as a substitute for coffee; young leaves make a good salad.

# BALM OF GILEAD
*Cedronella canariensis*

This perennial is usually grown as an annual. It has a musky scent that is used in potpourris. The bitter leaves can be brewed for tea.

❀ ☼

**GROW** Sow seed under cover in a sunny spot and plant out when all danger of frost is past. It needs good drainage but plenty of moisture during the growing season. The plant flowers late in the season.
**HARVEST** Pick leaves before the plant flowers for the best flavor; they can be used fresh or dried.
**COOK** Add the leaves to tea blends.

**HABIT** Upright, shrubby
↕ 5 ft (1.5 m) ↔ 3 ft (1 m)

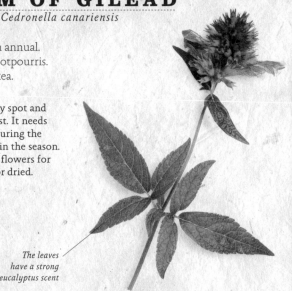

The leaves have a strong eucalyptus scent

# EDIBLE CHRYSANTHEMUM
*Chrysanthemum coronarium*

The bitter leaves and flowers of this annual are widely used as a flavoring in cooking in Asia, especially in China and Japan.

❀ ❀ ❀ ☼

**GROW** Sow seed in spring, in moist soil in full sun. Water frequently.
**HARVEST** Take leaves here and there all summer. Pick flowers as they appear to use fresh, let some flowers dry on the stem and crumble them to store.
**COOK** Add petals to salads, or blanch flower heads for one minute and serve with a savory sauce. Use young leaves and stems in stir-fries, stews, and soups.

**HABIT** Upright, branching
↕ 36 in (90 cm) ↔ 16 in (40 cm)

Petals, or the entire flower head can be used in cooking

# CILANTRO
## *Coriandrum sativum*

The leaves of this annual herb have a slightly pungent citrussy flavor, while the seeds have a sweet, warm, woody fragrance.

❀❀❀☼

**GROW** Sow seed in rich, moist soil in a protected sunny spot. If you want seeds as well as leaves, do not deadhead the flowers, and leave the seeds to ripen from green to light brown in color.

**HARVEST** Pick leaves all summer. Pick seedheads and dry fully before storing the seeds.

**COOK** Use fresh chopped leaves in salads, with coconut, citrus, avocado, fish, and meat. The dried seeds are spicy, sweet, and mildly orange-flavored—use them in curries and Asian dishes.

**HABIT** Upright, bushy
↕ 6–28 in (15–70 cm) ↔ 4–12 in (10–30 cm)

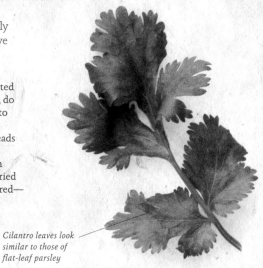

*Cilantro leaves look similar to those of flat-leaf parsley*

# CUMIN
## *Cuminum cyminum*

An ancient annual herb, today it is grown and used worldwide. The seeds of this delicate plant have a rich earthy flavor, so use them sparingly.

❀☼

**GROW** Sow seed in good, moist soil in full sun. Keep the plants well watered as drought can prevent them setting seed. Cumin is a floppy, thin-stemmed plant that grows best when draped over a support frame of chicken wire.

**HARVEST** Pick leaves as needed. When the plant browns and the seeds are dry, cut the stems and hang them to dry completely. Collect the seeds as they are released (see p116).

**COOK** Use the leaves in salads and spicy dishes. Once ground, dried seeds are pungent, sharp, and indispensable in Middle Eastern and Asian dishes. Cumin is often used with cilantro and chickpeas.

**HABIT** Slender, upright
↕ 6–12 in (15–30 cm) ↔ 3–4 in (8–10 cm)

*The delicate, floppy stems need some support in summer*

# CITRUS
*Citrus* spp.

Even in cold areas you can have a taste of the Mediterranean. These four perennial citrus plants will thrive on the patio in summer and indoors in winter. Their zest and juices add a tart flavor to both sweet and savory dishes.

❄ ☼

**GROW** Plant woody shrubs or trees in generous pots of rich, sandy, well-drained soil that can be moved to a bright place indoors when the freezing weather arrives. Buy young plants at the nursery that are on dwarfing rootstock. Keep them in full sun and water regularly, but give them a steady supply of nitrogen by watering with liquid fertilizer. Root prune and re-pot them after 4–5 years.
**HARVEST** Citrus fruits store well on the tree; pick as needed.
**COOK** Use dried peel to flavor stews, desserts, and sweet sauces. Add candied peel to cakes.

**ORANGE ▲**
*Citrus sinensis*
The flowers and, of course, the fruits have a strong orange aroma. Some varieties can be tart or bitter. Navel oranges have the best flavor; they are seedless with a navel-like formation at one end.
**HABIT** Upright tree
↕ 15–20 ft (4.5–6.1 m) ↔ 12–15 ft (3.6–4.5 m)
**COOK'S NOTES** Use flowers in teas and tisanes, and the zest and juice of the fruit in stews, with duck, and in desserts.

**KUMQUAT ▶**
*Fortunella japonica*
This compact plant produces small, slightly bitter, oval, orange fruits. Plant the superior-flavored variety *Fortunella crassifolia* 'Meiwa' if you can find it.
**HABIT** Medium-sized, bushy shrub
↕ 6–15 ft (1.8–4.5 m)
↔ 10–12 ft (3–3.6 m)
**COOK'S NOTES** Stew the yellow to red-orange fruits in Middle Eastern savory dishes, such as tagines.

*The fruits produce an aromatic rind as well as juice and flesh that can be used in sweet and savory dishes*

## LIME ▶

*Citrus aurantiifolia*

This small tree produces round green fruits with a pleasantly sour taste in late summer. Bearss lime (*Citrus* x *latifolia*) is a good variety. The leaves of the kaffir lime (*Citrus hystrix*) are used in Thai cooking.

**HABIT** Open structure
↕ 10–15 ft (3–5 m)
↔ 6–10 ft (2–3 m)

**COOK'S NOTES** Limes go well with herbs and spices such as ginger, cilantro, parsley, dill, and fenugreek. Add to chicken, fish, and lamb dishes.

*Fruits have a zingy zest but slightly sour, sharp-tasting flesh*

## LEMON ▶

*Citrus limon*

These are popular pot plants, which bear white, highly scented flowers and yellow, sharp-tasting fruits. A reliable, easy-to-grow and compact variety is 'Meyer Lemon', which will flower all year.

**HABIT** Medium-sized shrub
↕ 4–6 ft (1.2–1.8 m) in a generous pot
↔ 4–5 ft (1.2–1.5 m)

**COOK'S NOTES** The juice is good in salad dressings and desserts. The fruit can be used fresh or preserved, with roast poultry, in vegetable dishes, or with fish or grilled meats.

*Preserve whole lemons in salt and use the rind in stews and tagines*

# LEMONGRASS
### *Cymbopogon citratus*

This tropical, evergreen, perennial grass contains the same volatile oil as lemon rind, and so the stems impart a fresh, clean, citrussy flavor.

❉ ☼

**GROW** Sow seed in pots indoors in spring or divide established plants. Plant young plants outdoors in a sunny spot in good, moist soil. In temperate climates, grow in a generous pot. Lemongrass copes well outdoors during the summer, but take it indoors for the cold months.
**HARVEST** Cut the fresh leaves and lower stems of single stalks as needed.
**COOK** Fresh stems and leaves add a distinctive flavor to Thai curries and South East Asian dishes, such as salads, spring rolls, and fish dishes.

**HABIT** Clump-forming, with cane-like stems
↕ 4 ft (1.2 m) ↔ 3 ft (1 m)

*The stems and bases can be stored, whole, in a plastic bag in the fridge or frozen*

# MEADOWSWEET
### *Filipendula ulmaria*

Dense panicles of fragrant white flowers earn this perennial herb a place in ornamental gardens. The flowers and leaves are cucumber flavored.

❉ ❉ ❉ ♦ ☼

**GROW** Sow seed indoors in late winter for setting out in mid-spring, or divide established plants in fall. Meadowsweet is a marsh plant that needs a constantly wet, neutral to slightly alkaline soil and semi-shade. Avoid the cultivar 'Plena', as it is prone to mildew.
**HARVEST** You can pick flowers throughout the summer but take the leaves in mid-summer only.
**COOK** Traditionally used to make beer, the fresh flowers and crushed leaves also add a delicate, mild flavor to jams, stews, and drinks.

**HABIT** Clump-forming
↕ 2–4 ft (60 cm–1.2 m) ↔ 18 in (45 cm)

*Pick flowers just as they open and use fresh or dry*

# ARUGULA
*Eruca vesicaria* subsp. *sativa*

The arugula family includes many different varieties; most are edible herbs, but some are preferred for fragrance. Here are a few good culinary types.

**GROW** Sow seed in early spring in pots or directly in well-drained soil. Water well during the growing season. Arugula runs to seed quickly; don't let plants flower unless you want them to self-seed. Be warned, slugs and snails also love to eat the leaves.

**HARVEST** The leaves are ready before the hot weather arrives. Pick a few at a time, and leave the others to grow on.

**COOK** Add raw, whole leaves to salads. Use the leaves when young, as they become bitter with age.

*Fragrant flower heads make this a welcome addition to the garden*

## ◀ WILD ARUGULA
*Diplotaxis muralis*

This annual enjoys any good soil. The dandelion-like leaves have a bitter, peppery flavor.
**HABIT** Upright, leafy
↕ 12–18 in (30–45 cm)
↔ 10–12 in (25–30 cm)
**COOK'S NOTES** Use sparingly in mixed leaf salads, chop and add to soups and cooked dishes, or pair with chickpeas.

## SWEET ARUGULA ▶
*Hesperis matronalis*

This biennial herb is grown for its fragrant flower heads, which, like its bitter leaves, are also edible.
**HABIT** Upright, leafy
↕ 24–36 in (60–90 cm)
↔ 12–18 in (30–45 cm)
**COOK'S NOTES** Use leaves and flowers in salads.

## ARUGULA ▶
*Eruca vesicaria* subsp. *sativa*

This annual tolerates dappled shade as well as full sun. Keep soil moist.
**HABIT** Upright, leafy
↕ 6–10 in (15–25 cm)
↔ 8–12 in (20–30 cm)
**COOK'S NOTES** Use young leaves in salads, or cook as you would spinach.

# FENNEL
*Foeniculum vulgare*

Do not confuse this perennial herb with
Florence fennel, a bulbous-based vegetable.
This herb is grown for its licorice-flavored
leaves and seeds.

✾✾✾☼

**GROW** Sow seed in spring. Fennel is happy in most
well-drained soils as long as it has full sun. It is a
tall, aromatic plant, which bears an abundant crop
of seeds each year. Water well until established. In
fall, cut the stems to 1 in (2.5 cm) above the ground;
they will return in spring.
**HARVEST** Cut stalks and leaves in early summer
before the stems turn woody. Harvest seedheads for
drying when they are yellow-green.
**COOK** Use the leaves in marinades for pork,
chicken, and lamb, or in salad dressings. Use seeds
or fronds with sea bass or oily fish such as salmon.

**BRONZE
FENNEL ▶**
*Foeniculum vulgare*
'Purpureum'
Pick leaves early in the
season, and let new
growth ripen over the
summer. It is shorter and
less vigorous than ordinary
fennel, with a milder licorice flavor.
**HABIT** Tall, upright stems
↕ 3–5 ft (90 cm–1.5 m) ↔ 10–12 in (25–30 cm)
**COOK'S NOTES** Use seeds and leaves in vinegar,
tea, breads, cakes, pies, and sausages.
Sprouting seeds are good in salads.

**◀ GREEN FENNEL**
*Foeniculum vulgare*
Don't plant near dill or they may hybridize. Replant
every 3–4 years. A graceful plant with feathery
leaves and a licorice flavor throughout.
**HABIT** Tall, upright stems
↕ 5–6 ft (1.5–1.8 m) ↔ about 12 in (30 cm)

# SWEET WOODRUFF
### *Galium odoratum*

A pretty, perennial groundcover plant with profuse, tiny white flowers. The flowers, stems, and leaves all have a delicate vanilla flavor.

✿✿✿☀

**GROW** Sow seed in well-drained soil in spring. It prefers semi-shade to full shade, which makes it useful under and around shrubs. It self-sows freely once established.

**HARVEST** Cut and dry flowers and leaves together in early summer.

**COOK** Traditionally used to prepare punches and wine cups, such as May wine in Germany, and in cocktails. Sprinkle tiny flowers on salads, but use sparingly. Brew a calming tea with the leaves.

**HABIT** Creeping
‡ 20 in (50 cm) ↔ indefinite

*The aroma of the plant is strengthened when it is wilted or dried*

# HOPS
### *Humulus lupulus*

Hops are well-known for flavoring beer, and the female flowers of this perennial vine are also used to make tea. The stems can be steamed.

✿✿✿☀

**GROW** Plant young plants in rich soil in full sun. With regular water, the common hop will cover a massive amount of aerial space. Because it grows so fast, you need to enrich deep soil with plenty of compost to nourish it. It will need a large arbor, extensive trellis, or an open tree to grow into.

**HARVEST** Pick young, fresh side shoots in spring. Collect the female flowers—tiered flaky bracts with tiny flowers between them—while fresh and green, and the male flowers as needed.

**COOK** Blanch young shoots and serve hot as spring greens, or use in soups or salads. Parboil male flowers and add to salads when cold.

**HABIT** Climbing
‡ 10–20 ft (3–6 m) ↔ indefinite

*The male flowers grow in yellowish clusters and can be cooked*

# HYSSOP
*Hyssopus officinalis*

The leaves and flowers of this perennial herb
have a strong, minty, slightly bitter flavor.
In mild winter areas the leaves are evergreen.

❋ ❋ ❋ ☼

**GROW** Sow seed indoors in late winter. Transplant
to pots by early spring, and set out in a sunny spot
in the garden by mid-spring. Hyssop tolerates dry
soil but does better when watered as needed. Trim
the top shoots to encourage bushy growth.

**HARVEST** In some areas leaves can be picked year
round. Cut flowers in summer when they are
fully open.

**COOK** Add the pungent fresh flowers to fruit dishes
and salads sparingly, and use the powerful leaves in
moderation in pies, and meat or game dishes.

**HABIT** Dwarf shrub
↕ 18–24 in (45–60 cm) ↔ 3 ft (90 cm)

*The leaves release
their aroma when
brushed against,
which makes it a good
plant for hedging*

# JASMINE
*Jasminum officinale*

This perennial climber emits one of the most
exotic perfumes in the world, and its highly
scented flowers can be used in cooking.

❋ ❋ ❋ ☼ ☼

**GROW** Buy young vines at the nursery and plant
them in well-drained soil against a wall, fence, or
trellis. Jasmine can withstand temperatures down
to 30°F (-1°C). The vine blooms best with full
sun, regular watering, and rich soil, but
tolerates some shade.

**HARVEST** Pick the blossoms just before
they open, from summer until early fall.

**COOK** Use the flowers fresh in infusion for tea,
and occasionally desserts.

**HABIT** Climbing
↕ 30 ft (10 m) ↔ indefinite

*Pick flowers
while still buds*

# JUNIPER
### *Juniperus communis*

Often found in borders, these perennial shrubs have prickly evergreen leaves and bear their edible piney-flavored berries year round.

❊❊❊☼◐

**GROW** Sow seed or grow from cuttings in spring or fall, or buy a plant of modest size. Juniper grows in any well-drained soil. Position in full sun in cold regions, or partial shade where summers are hot. They need no fertilizing, but water occasionally in dry summers. They do not like boggy soil.

**HARVEST** Pick berries when they are dark, almost black, with a bluish bloom in late summer.

**COOK** Berries traditionally flavor gin and other spirits. To enjoy their flavor in food, crush them and use in marinades, meat stews, pot roasts, stuffings, and winter cabbage dishes. Use fresh, dried, or frozen.

**HABIT** Upright, spreading or prostrate shrub
↕ 6–12 ft (2–4 m) ↔ 6–12 ft (2–4 m)

Harvest the
berries when
they are
almost black

# BAY LEAF
### *Laurus nobilis*

The ancients crowned victors with wreaths of bay leaves; today cooks have many uses for them. This evergreen shrub bears bitter leaves all year.

❊❊☼

**GROW** Sow seed in spring or buy young plants. In cooler regions, plant in a generous pot that can be moved indoors during the winter. If planting in the garden it will tolerate any soil as long as it is well drained, in full sun, and sheltered from cold, drying winds. The plant will withstand summer droughts. Prune it back if you want to create a smaller shrub.

**HARVEST** Pick dark green, leathery leaves any time.

**COOK** Mix with thyme and parsley to make a bouquet garni; allow to dry a little or use frozen leaves in meat stews, poultry and fish dishes, and custards. Do not store beyond 3–4 months or the leaves lose their aroma.

**HABIT** Dense tree
↕ 10–50 ft (3–15 m) ↔ 30 ft (10 m)

Fresh leaves have
a stronger flavor
than dried ones

# LAVENDER
*Lavandula* spp.

The sweetly camphorous scent of this perennial defines freshness. The flowers have the strongest scent, but you can also use the leaves in cooking.

**GROW** These are good drought-tolerant plants once established, so plant young plants or cuttings in poor, sandy, dry soils in full sun where they will produce more of their aromatic oils. Deadhead faded flowers in late summer and cut back the plant to within an inch or so of the older stems in fall (see p96). Do not cut into the woody part of the stem or it will kill the plant.

**HARVEST** Pick flower heads and cut stems when the flowers first open. Harvest leaves at any time.

**COOK** Use in moderation. Flowers add flavor to desserts, ice cream, sugar, cookies such as shortbread, and drinks. Leaves make a good alternative to rosemary in stews and stuffings.

*Tall, fragrant flower heads rise above bushy growth*

*Violet bracts appear almost year round in warmer climates*

### ◄ FRENCH LAVENDER
*Lavandula dentata*

❄ ☼

The short, gray-green, aromatic, evergreen leaves have a more pungent, camphor note than English lavender.
**HABIT** Upright shrub
↕ 12–24 in (30–60 cm)
↔ 12–18 in (30–45 cm)

*Short evergreen leaves have a pungent note*

### ENGLISH LAVENDER ▲
*Lavandula angustifolia*

❄ ❄ ❄ ☼

The most aromatic of the lavenders, with a milder, more floral scent than the intense Mediterranean lavenders. Don't fertilize and don't overwater.
**HABIT** Upright shrub
↕ 12–24 in (30–60 cm)
↔ 12–18 in (30–45 cm)

# LOVAGE
*Levisticum officinale*

This perennial herb has a sharp, penetrating, celery-like flavor throughout its seeds, stalks, and leaves, so only cook with small quantities.

❋ ❋ ❋ ☼ ◐

**GROW** Sow seed indoors in late winter. Set out started plants in good garden soil in a protected spot once all risk of frost has passed. They will need adequate water and protection from full sun in the hottest regions. Divide plants in spring or fall.

**HARVEST** Pick leaves and stalks in summer. Harvest seedheads by cutting down stems when the seeds start to turn brown, then dry (see p116).

**COOK** Young shoots can be eaten raw or blanched as a spring vegetable. Add chopped leaves to salads, soups, stews, and stocks for a strong, aromatic, celery flavor.

**HABIT** Low-growing mound with tall stems
↕ 6 ft (2 m) ↔ 3 ft (1 m)

*Use lovage seed in cooking as you would celery seed*

# LEMON BALM
*Melissa officinalis*

The highly aromatic leaves of this perennial give the impression of lemon with a hint of mint. The flowers are also much loved by bees.

❋ ❋ ❋ ☼ ◐

**GROW** Divide plants in fall or spring, or sow seed in spring in any good soil in a sunny spot; in very hot regions it will need some shade. Lemon balm self-sows with abandon and will be a pest if not controlled.

**HARVEST** Pick young leaves throughout the summer and use them fresh, because the flavor is delicate and fades as the leaves age and when dried.

**COOK** Use fresh baby leaves to add a delicate lemon-mint flavor to tea, and fruit and wine drinks. Chop and mix with soft cheeses.

**HABIT** Upright, bushy
↕ 24 in (60 cm) ↔ 18 in (45 cm)

*The leaves look like mint, but release a citrussy scent when crushed*

# BERGAMOT
### *Monarda didyma*

This pretty perennial has a place in both the ornamental and herb garden. The aromatic leaves and flowers both have culinary uses.

✿✿✿💧☼☀

**GROW** Sow seed indoors in late winter or directly in the garden from early spring to mid-summer, or grow from cuttings in early summer. It likes good, well-drained garden soil and full sun to dappled shade. Its volatile oils make it resistant to insect damage. Divide plants in early spring (see p91).

**HARVEST** The hot, high summer days are the best time to pick leaves and flowers.

**COOK** Use fresh leaves when brewing tea or add them to stuffings for pork and poultry. Scatter the flower petals over salads.

**HABIT** Upright, bushy
↕ 3–4 ft (90 cm–1.2 m) ↔ 12–24 in (30–60 cm)

# CURRY LEAF
### *Murraya koenigii*

This small, perennial tree can only be grown outdoors in the tropics, but you can grow it indoors elsewhere for its musky, citrussy leaves.

✿☼

**GROW** In tropical climates, sow seed directly into rich garden soil or grow from semi-ripe cuttings in late spring or early summer. Elsewhere, sow in pots in a hot, sunny spot indoors. Water well, as it is a thirsty plant.

**HARVEST** Fresh leaves are available most of the year, except for during a short winter spell. They freeze well in freezer bags.

**COOK** Use fresh, dried, or from frozen in vegetarian curries, with pork, or in stuffings for samosas.

**HABIT** Tall shrub or small tree
↕ 20 ft (6 m) ↔ 10–15 ft (3–5 m)

# SWEET CICELY
## *Myrrhis odorata*

The ferny foliage and white flowers of this hardy perennial carry a light licorice scent, leading some to call it Great Chervil. All parts are edible.

✲ ✲ ✲ ☼

**GROW** Sow seed in fall directly in the garden, or grow from root cuttings in spring or fall. This plant prefers light shade and humusy soil, as you would find in the woods. Best for the shady part of the herb garden; if planted in sun, its leaves yellow and die in summer, returning in fall.

**HARVEST** Stalks, stems, and leaves can all be harvested at any time. Collect fresh seeds when they are green, ripe seeds to dry when dark brown.

**COOK** Stew leaves with fruit to reduce tartness, or add to salads and egg dishes. Use fresh seeds in ice cream and fruit salads, dried seeds in desserts, and grate the root or cook as a vegetable.

**HABIT** Large, open
↕ 1–2m (3–6ft) ↔ 60cm–1.2m (2–4ft)

*The fern-like leaves smell of licorice when crushed*

# MYRTLE
## *Myrtus communis*

The leaves and flower buds of this perennial shrub are spicy with fragrant flowers. Like juniper, the seeds can be ground as a spice.

✲ ✲ ☼

**GROW** Take softwood cuttings in spring and semi-hardwood ones in summer and grow on in pots or out in the garden. It prefers well-drained soil of medium fertility in full sun. Myrtle needs little care and can withstand summer droughts.

**HARVEST** Pick leaves, unopened flower buds, open flowers, and berries as they appear in summer.

**COOK** Add the flower buds to salads (without the green parts) and use the berries for their gently resinous orange-blossom flavor. Dry and grind the berries in a pestle and mortar before using.

**HABIT** Dense, mounded shrub
↕ 5–6 ft (1.5–1.8 m) ↔ 4–5 ft (1.2–1.5 m)

# MINT
*Mentha* spp.

This perennial herb is grown everywhere and is used to flavor just about anything. Spearmint and peppermint are the two most popular kinds, but there are many others.

✿✿✿◆☼

**GROW** Sow seed in spring, or take root cuttings or divide clumps. Mint likes rich, wet soil, full sun, or dappled shade in hot regions. Mint spreads rapidly by underground rhizomes, so keep plants in check by planting them in pots.
**HARVEST** Pick leaves or whole stems when young and fresh.
**COOK** Mints have a dominant flavor, so use sparingly with other herbs to enhance delicate ingredients. The flavored varieties have subtle aromas, which evaporate quickly: add them to lamb, dairy, and vegetable dishes, and fruit and chocolate desserts at the last minute.

## MOROCCAN MINT ▶
*Mentha spicata* var. *crispa* 'Moroccan'
Best grown away from other mints, as this mint hybridizes easily. It has a clean, slightly spicy, mint flavor.
**HABIT** Upright, bushy
↕ 12–18 in (30–45 cm)
↔ 24–36 in (60–90 cm)
**COOK'S NOTES** Use in all dishes needing mint, and for brewing tea.

## SPEARMINT ▶
*Mentha spicata*
Has a clean flavor but loses potency after flowering. Cut back to 6–8 in (15–20 cm) to promote new growth. Divide clumps.
**HABIT** Upright, spreading
↕ 10–18 in (25–45 cm) or more
↔ 24–36 in (60–90 cm) or more
**COOK'S NOTES** Serve very fresh sprigs with tarragon with barbecued meats.

*Mint family members have square stems*

Stems and leaf veins are reddish-purple when grown in good, moist soil

### ◄ CHOCOLATE MINT

*Mentha x piperita f. citrata* 'Chocolate'
The dark green to purple leaves have a distinct chocolate-mint smell.
**HABIT** Upright, bushy
↕ 12–18 in (30–45 cm)
↔ 24–36 in (60–90 cm)
**COOK'S NOTES** Add to ice creams, chocolate desserts, and berries. Particularly good with raspberries.

### APPLE MINT ►

*Mentha suaveolens*
A vigorous plant with downy leaves that have a slight apple aroma.
**HABIT** Spreading
↕ 18–24 in (45–60 cm)
↔ 24–36 in (60–90 cm) or more
**COOK'S NOTES** Good for flavoring cider vinegar, and adding to sauces.

### GINGER MINT ▲

*Mentha x gracilis* (syn. *M. x gentilis*)
A hardy perennial with a delicate, warm flavor.
**HABIT** Spreading
↕ 18–24 in (45–60 cm)
↔ 24–36 in (60–90 cm) or more

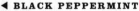

Slightly hairy leaves have a strong peppermint scent

### ◄ BLACK PEPPERMINT

*Mentha x piperita* var. *piperita*
'Black Peppermint'
This is a choice variety with dark purple stems and dark green, oval, strongly peppermint-scented leaves.
**HABIT** Spreading
↕ 18–24 in (45–60 cm)
↔ 24–36 in (60–90 cm) or more
**COOK'S NOTES** Use sparingly in desserts, or in teas.

### PEPPERMINT ►

*Mentha x piperita*
A tall-growing hybrid with a strong minty flavor.
**HABIT** Spreading
↕ 24 in (60cm) ↔ 36 in (90 cm) or more

# CRESSES
*Nasturtium*

The cresses listed here are not aromatic but have a pleasant, crisp, peppery flavor in their leaves and their succulent stems.

**GROW** Sow seed in pots or in garden soil in early spring. Both varieties like a sunny spot.
**HARVEST** Cut the leaves as required.
**COOK** The leaves of both cresses give a peppery flavor to salads and make a good garnish.

### GARDEN CRESS ▶
*Lepidium sativum*
❀❀❀☼

This annual herb grows from seed to very spicy, peppery cress in just a week in ordinary garden soil and is ready to harvest a few weeks later. Often planted with mustard seed to produce lively micro-greens.
**HABIT** Low growing
↕ 3 in (7.5 cm) ↔ indefinite
**COOK'S NOTES** Use in sandwiches and as a peppery finish to dishes and salads.

### WATERCRESS ▶
*Nasturtium officinale*
❀❀❀◗☼

Sow seed in alkaline soil. It will grow in pots or the garden if the soil is kept constantly wet. Pick the stems in late spring/early summer.
**HABIT** Low-growing, sprawling
↕ 8–10 in (20–25 cm) ↔ indefinite
**COOK'S NOTES** Wilt florets in pan juices and serve them with meat; or use in soups and savory tarts.

# PERILLA
### *Perilla* spp.

This annual herb is better known as shiso in Japan and much of Asia. The decorative leaves have a spicy scent that is reminiscent of cinnamon and cloves.

❀ ❀ ☼

**GROW** This herb must be grown as an annual, as it doesn't withstand frost. Sow seed in spring indoors in pots or outdoors in a sunny spot and well-drained soil once all risk of frost has passed. Give plants a mid-summer drink of liquid fertilizer. Move pots indoors in winter or if frost is forecast.

**HARVEST** Pick leaves or growing tips here and there at any time.

**COOK** Add fresh to noodle soups, spring rolls, and fish, rice, and vegetable dishes.

**◀ GREEN PERILLA**
*Perilla frutescens* var. *crispa*
The green variety does not like to be waterlogged. Pinch out the growing tips to force more of the leaves. The flavor is more potent than in the red variety.
**HABIT** Upright, bushy
↕ 24–36 in (60–90 cm)
↔ 24 in (60 cm)
**COOK'S NOTES** It is used as a vegetable in Japanese cuisine.

*The pretty, frilly red leaves look good in food and the garden*

**PURPLE PERILLA ▶**
*Perilla frutescens* var. *purpurascens*
The red variety is not as vigorous as the green one, nor as potent, but it does self-sow readily. Gather seed to sow the next spring.
**HABIT** Upright, bushy
↕ 24 in (60 cm) ↔ 12 in (30 cm)
**COOK'S NOTES** Use in cake mixes and drinks or as a dye when pickling vegetables.

# BASIL
*Ocimum* spp.

Basil is one of the must-have annual herbs to grow in or for the kitchen. The cinnamon-licorice-mint aroma and flavor of its leaves contributes to many cuisines around the world.

✤ ✤ ✤ ☼

**GROW** Sow seed in spring and throughout the summer in well-drained soil or pots. It likes full sun and adequate moisture. The plant stops growing leaves and loses flavor when it flowers, so pinch out flower buds as they appear. Give the plant a mid-summer feed of liquid fertilizer.

**HARVEST** Pick young stems with their shiny leaves as they are needed.

**COOK** The tomato, of course, is basil's perfect partner. Basil's flavor intensifies when cooked, for a more subtle taste, use it raw or add it at the end of cooking.

*Keep a pot of bas in the kitchen; th scent of the leave repels flies*

**SWEET BASIL ▶**
*Ocimum basilicum*
A strongly scented variety with large, bright green leaves.
**HABIT** Upright, bushy
↕ 2–2½ ft (60–75 cm) ↔ 2 ft (60 cm)
**COOK'S NOTES** Use in pesto, salads, tomato sauces, and soups.

**GREEK BASIL ▶**
*Ocimum minimum* 'Greek'
This easy-to-grow variety has the smallest leaves of all, but they still have a good flavor.
**HABIT** Compact, bushy
↕ 6–12 in (15–30 cm)
↔ 6–12 in (15–30 cm)
**COOK'S NOTES** Add whole leaves to salads and tomato sauces.

**LEMON BASIL ▶**
*Ocimum* x *citriodorum*
Both the leaves and flowers of this variety have a fresh, clean, lemony scent.
**HABIT** Compact, bushy
↕ 18 in (45 cm)
↔ 12–24 in (30–60 cm)
**COOK'S NOTES** It is excellent in tomato salads and fish stews.

### ◀ PURPLE RUFFLES BASIL
*Ocimum basilicum* var. *purpurascens* 'Purple Ruffles'

Similar to Purple Basil but this variety has less flavor. It is tricky to raise from seed.
**HABIT** Upright, bushy
↕ 24–30 in (60–75 cm)
↔ 24 in (60 cm)

*The large leaves have a ruffled, frilly appearance*

### THAI BASIL ▶
*Ocimum basilicum* 'Horapha'

The leaves carry a sweet licorice and peppery aroma and a strong licorice flavor.
**HABIT** Sturdy, compact, bushy
↕ 12–18 in (30–45 cm)
↔ 12 in (30 cm)
**COOK'S NOTES** Much-used in Thailand, add sparingly to curries.

### HOLY BASIL ▲
*Ocimum sanctum*

The green leaves have a spicy aroma. It originates in Thailand, where it is grown around Buddhist temples.
**HABIT** Vigorous, upright
↕ 18–24 in (45–60 cm) ↔ 24 in (60 cm)
**COOK'S NOTES** A staple ingredient in Thai cooking, such as in stir-fries with chicken, beef, or pork.

*The leaves release a strong cinnamon scent when bruised*

### ◀ CINNAMON BASIL
*Ocimum basilicum* 'Cinnamon'

Native to Mexico, this basil has clear cinnamon notes.
**HABIT** Upright, bushy
↕ 12–24 in (30–60 cm)
↔ 18 in (45 cm)
**COOK'S NOTES** Tear leaves and add to South American dishes, and use in desserts.

### PURPLE BASIL ▲
*Ocimum basilicum* var. *purpurascens*

A striking plant with its dark maroon-purple, almost black leaves. The leaves have a distinct clove and mint flavor.
**HABIT** Upright, bushy
↕ 2–2½ ft (60–75 cm) ↔ 24 in (60 cm)
**COOK'S NOTES** Use to flavor oils and butter, and as a garnish.

# OREGANO AND MARJORAM
*Origanum* spp.

These herbs are different species in the same genus. Their aromatic leaves are delicious in cooking. Both are perennials, but marjoram is often grown as an annual in cold-winter areas.

**GROW** Sow seed in pots in early spring or in the garden in mid-spring in full sun. You can increase plants by root division (see p90). Do not enrich the soil or feed the plants; a poor soil forces the plant to produce more of the volatile oils that give the leaves their aroma and flavor.

**HARVEST** Pick leaves at any time, but they are at their finest just before flowering.

**COOK** Their pungent, spicy flavor gives a unique lift to Mediterranean ingredients and dishes—pizza, pasta, fish, meat, beans, tomatoes, eggplant, and zucchini.

*Greek oregano has dark green leaves that are slightly hairy*

### OREGANO ▲
*Origanum vulgare*
✿✿✿☼

The stems often flop when the flower heads mature. Cut back after flowering to prevent straggly growth. Use fresh or frozen for maximum impact. Oregano keeps its peppery flavor well when dried, too.
**HABIT** Bushy
‡ 24–36 in (60–90 cm) ↔ 3–4 ft (90 cm–1.2 m)

### ◄ GREEK OREGANO
*Origanum vulgare* subsp. *hirtum* 'Greek'
✿✿✿☼

The dark green leaves have a strong, resinous aroma and are excellent for cooking.
**HABIT** Bushy
‡ 24 in (60 cm) ↔ 24–36 in (60–90 cm)
**COOK'S NOTES** Good for rich stews and pasta dishes.

**◀ POT MARJORAM**
*Origanum onites*

❋ ❋ ☼

This variety will grow as a perennial when planted in full sun. Allow the soil to dry before watering. This has a less sweet, more piquant flavor than other varieties.
**HABIT** Small, shrubby
↕ 12–24 in (30–60 cm)
↔ 12–24 in (30–60 cm)
**COOK'S NOTES** Rub on meats before roasting, add to pasta, or sprinkle on cheese, egg, and vegetable dishes.

*The aromatic leaves form a pretty, dense mat in winter*

*Round, fuzzy leaves release milder aromas and flavors*

**SWEET MARJORAM ▲**
*Origanum majorana*

❋ ☼

The curving stems don't grow as tall as those of common oregano, and the leaves have a more delicate, sweet flavor. Mulch with straw to prevent stems lolling.
**HABIT** Shrubby
↕ 12–24 in (30–60 cm) ↔ 12–24 in (30–60 cm)

**DITTANY OF CRETE ▶**
*Origanum dictamnus*

❋ ❋ ☼

Short stems produce woolly-looking leaves that are unlike other oreganos and have a milder aroma and flavor. The arching stems look best in hanging baskets or elevated pots.
**HABIT** Low growing
↕ 8 in (20 cm) ↔ 12–24 in (30–60 cm)
**COOK'S NOTES** Used to make tea in Crete. It is good with grilled fish.

# SCENTED GERANIUM
*Pelargonium* spp.

Despite their common name, pelargoniums are not related to true geraniums; instead they are perennial herbs with woody stems. Some of these have edible leaves, which have a variety of aromas.

❋ ☼

**GROW** Plant young plants or cuttings in good garden soil enriched with compost in full sun in spring, once all risk of frost has passed. The plants die back in frost, so it is a good idea to plant them in pots that can be moved indoors in cold weather. Pinch out faded blossoms to encourage new blooms. Take cuttings in fall.

**HARVEST** Pick individual leaves from plants any time during the growing season.

**COOK** Use the leaves to flavor preserves, syrups, teas, butters, and sorbets. As with bay, remove the leaves before serving.

*The leaves of this variety have the most delicate scent*

**LEMON-SCENTED GERANIUM ▶**

*Pelargonium crispum*

Its divided leaves release a lemon aroma when crushed. Keep well watered during hot, dry spells.

**HABIT** Upright, neat
‡ 12–36 in (30–90 cm)
↔ 12–36 in (30–90 cm)

**PRINCE OF ORANGE GERANIUM ▶**

*Pelargonium 'Prince of Orange'*

Produces orange-scented, green, crinkled leaves. Pretty in herb gardens and at the front of ornamental borders. Pinch tips to promote bushy growth.

**HABIT** Upright, leafy
‡ 12–36 in (30–90 cm)
↔ 12–36 in (30–90 cm)

**ROSE-SCENTED GERANIUM ▲**

*Pelargonium graveolens*

Very finely divided leaves. There are many rose-scented geraniums, but this one has the softest scent of all. Give a mid-summer feeding of liquid fertilizer.

**HABIT** Upright, leafy
‡ 12–36 in (30–90 cm) ↔ 12–36 in (30–90 cm)

**COOK'S NOTES** Good for lining cake pans as an alternative, fragrant baking parchment. Infuse to make rose-scented syrup.

# PARSLEY
*Petroselinum* spp.

One of the most useful herbs, bearing nutritious leaves packed with flavor. This biennial is good in pots and makes an attractive edging plant.

❀❀☼◑

**GROW** This herb blooms in the second year, but the seed needs sowing in spring each year to produce plants in succession. Parsley favors rich, well-drained garden soil and a sunny or partially shaded spot. Enrich the soil around the plant with compost in mid-summer.

**HARVEST** Select whole stems, leaving plenty on each plant so they stay well nourished.

**COOK** Both the stems and leaves can be added to a multitude of savory dishes; from omelets to stews to baked fish. Parsley freezes well but is not worth drying.

*The delicate-looking leaves have a strong flavor*

**FLAT-LEAF PARSLEY ▼**
*Petroselinum crispum* var. *neapolitanum* 'Italian'
Soak seed in warm water for 24 hours before planting to hasten germination. It has a more pronounced flavor than the curly type.
**HABIT** Neat, bushy
↕ 24–36 in (60–90 cm)
↔ 12–36 in (30–60 cm)

*Sprigs look pretty as a garnish*

**▲CURLY PARSLEY**
*Petroselinum crispum*
If starting from seed, expect germination to take up to a month. It has a mild flavor.
**HABIT** Low-growing mound
↕ 10–12 in (25–30 cm) ↔ 12 in (30 cm)
**COOK'S NOTES** Chop finely if sprinkling on dishes as an edible garnish, as the tough curly leaves can be rough on the palate.

# ANISE
*Pimpinella anisum*

The leaves of this annual can be used as
flavoring, but it is the seeds that are most prized
for their rich, licorice flavor.

**GROW** Anise has a tap root and resents moving
once established, so in spring, sow seed in a light,
well-drained soil in full sun where you want it to
grow. It takes about four months from seedling
to seed-bearing, so it's not for regions that have
late frosts or prolonged cold weather. Water
infrequently but deeply.
**HARVEST** Just before the seeds ripen, cut the stalks
and hang them to dry in paper bags (see p116).
**COOK** Chop fresh leaves to add a spiced sweetness
to salads and fruit; seeds enhance breads, apple pies,
curries, fish stews, cakes, and dried fruit dishes.

**HABIT** Upright, leafy
‡ 20 in (50 cm) ↔ 10–18 in (24–45 cm)

# PURSLANE
*Portulaca oleracea*

This annual makes a good pot herb, or you can
use the leaves, stems, and flower buds to add
a snow pea-like flavor and texture to salads.

**GROW** Sow seed in any soil in full sun in spring.
Purslane grows quickly once the ground warms
up. If harvesting the herb from fields, make sure
no pesticides have been used. It does require some
additional water in hot summers.
**HARVEST** Pull up whole plants any time before the
flower buds open.
**COOK** Its flower buds, stems, and fleshy leaves make
a good ingredient in mixed salads. You can cook the
foliage as you would spinach, or chop them and add
to tabbouleh.

**HABIT** Trailing
‡ 8–18 in (20–45 cm) ↔ 18–24 in (45–60 cm)

*Purslane is
believed to be
a rich source
of omega-3
fatty acids*

# SUMAC
### *Rhus* spp.

In meadows, woodlands, and wastelands this perennial is a common shrub, which puts on a dramatic red-leafed display in fall. Either harvest berries or leave them to develop into seeds, which have a distinctive astringent quality.

**GROW** Sow seed in early spring in full sun to dappled shade. It is happy in poor soil, but grow it in moist but well-drained soil for the best fall color. Mulch seedlings to conserve moisture. The suckers from this shrub can be invasive.

**HARVEST** Cut off dense clusters of red-berried seedheads in the fall. Plant a few seeds directly and store the rest in paper bags (see p116).

**COOK** Use the seedheads whole, ground, or extract the juice after soaking to add a pleasantly sour, fruity flavor to Middle Eastern dishes. Dried seedheads make a calming tea and are good scattered over flat bread dough before baking.

## STAGHORN SUMAC ▶
*Rhus typhina*
❋ ❋ ❋ ☼ ◑
The branches are covered with downy hairs, hence its common name.
**HABIT** Upright, bushy
↕ 6–7 ft (1.8–2.1 m) ↔ 3–4 ft (90 cm–1.2 m)
**COOK'S NOTES** Its berries can be washed, strained, sweetened, and made into pink lemonade.

## SICILIAN SUMAC ▼
*Rhus coriaria*
❋ ❋ ☼
Grow it only in full sun, in dry or moist soil. This variety has the best flavored, tart berries of all the sumacs.
**HABIT** Upright, open, branching
↕ 10 ft (3 m) ↔ 5–6 ft (1.5–1.8 m)
**COOK'S NOTES** Its acidic berries are made into a condiment in the Middle East.

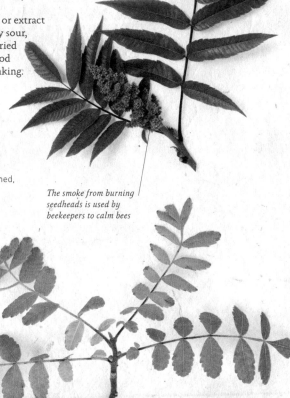

The smoke from burning seedheads is used by beekeepers to calm bees

# BLACK CURRANT
*Ribes nigrum*

The black fruits of this bushy, deciduous shrub have a slightly tart flavor and are a great source of vitamin C.

✲✲✲☼

**GROW** Plant young plants in a sunny part of the herb garden in good, well-drained soil. They are happy in cold winter areas. Mulch each shrub with rich compost in the spring before the buds form.
**HARVEST** Pick the ripe berries in mid-summer.
**COOK** Black currants are a perfect ingredient for ice cream, summer desserts, jams, preserves, cordials (see p175), and liqueurs.

**HABIT** Bushy shrub
↕ 4–5 ft (1.2–1.5 m) ↔ 4–5 ft (1.2–1.5 m)

# ROSE
*Rosa rugosa*

This is the perfect rose for the herb garden. This perennial produces fragrant blooms followed by large, tomato-red hips (seed pods).

✲✲✲☼

**GROW** Plant young plants in full sun in decent soil next to a fence, wall, trellis, or other support. This rose has good pest and disease resistance.
**HARVEST** Pick flowers as needed, but leave some to develop into hips. Collect the hips when they have reached a good size and have turned red.
**COOK** Use newly opened flowers to make rosewater and the flowers or hips to make syrup. Dried petals are ground for use in spice blends.

**HABIT** Rambling
↕ 3–6 ft (1–2 m) ↔ 3–6 ft (1–2 m)

*Do not deadhead faded flowers, to allow hips to develop*

# SORREL
*Rumex* spp.

This leafy herb adds a tangy, acidic flavor to soups and rich foods. There are two species of sorrel used as herbs—both are perennials.

✻✻✻☼

**GROW** Sow seed in rich, moist soil in a partially shaded spot; the leaves become bitter in full sun. Sorrel is quick to bolt, so remove flower stalks to encourage leaf growth.

**HARVEST** Pick leaves throughout the growing season while they are young. The leaves freeze well.

**COOK** Use fresh leaves in salads, sauces, soups, and in fish dishes. Sorrel is the perfect partner for butter and cream. Mature leaves can be acidic so are best used in moderation.

*The smaller, shield-shaped leaves have a succulent texture*

**GARDEN SORREL ▶**
*Rumex acetosa*
The common variety of sorrel makes a clump of tangy, sharp-flavored leaves that can be divided in fall.
**HABIT** Clump-forming, low growing
‡ 24–36 in (60–90 cm)
↔ 3–4 ft (90 cm–1.2 m)

*Sharp in flavor, the large dark leaves partner rich foods perfectly*

**◀ FRENCH SORREL**
*Rumex scutatus*
This species can take more sun than garden sorrel. The leaves have a milder, more lemony flavor and a succulent texture.
**HABIT** Clump-forming, low growing
‡ 6–10 in (15–25 cm)
↔ 24–36 in (60–90 cm)

# ROSEMARY
### *Rosmarinus officinalis*

These perennials come in different shapes and sizes; from tall upright ones to those that hug the ground. The edible flowers can be blue, white, and, rarely, pink. All have needle-like aromatic leaves with a sweet, resinous smell.

**GROW** Sow seed or plant cuttings in pots or in the garden in spring. Rosemary tolerates poor, dry soil, but it thrives in good soil. Do not overwater; rosemary will die in boggy or wet soil.

**HARVEST** Cut off the outer stems and pick flowers as needed.

**COOK** A quintessential flavor of Mediterranean cooking. Cut sprigs for casseroles or as skewers to grill food. Chop leaves or use them whole with meat, especially lamb, casseroles, potatoes, fish, rice, and breads, or infuse in vinegar and oil. Flowers have a milder flavor and look good in ice cubes.

### ROSEMARY ▶
*Rosmarinus officinalis*
❋ ❋ ☼
The common evergreen shrub has dark green, aromatic leaves.
**HABIT** Upright, bushy
↕ 5 ft (1.5 m) ↔ 5 ft (1.5 m)

*The stems have a strong flavor and a woody texture, so remove cooked sprigs before serving dishes*

### ◀ PROSTRATE ROSEMARY
*Rosmarinus officinalis* Prostratus Group
❋ ❋ ☼
A cascading form that will trail attractively over walls, down banks, and from hanging baskets. It has highly aromatic, strongly flavored leaves. Renew by division (see p91) every few years to prevent dead centers.
**HABIT** Trailing
↕ 10–24 in (25–60 cm)
↔ 4–8 ft (1.2–2.4 m)

**ROSEMARY 'MAJORCA PINK'** ▶
*Rosmarinus officinalis* 'Majorca Pink'
❋ ☼

Tall branches flop into an interesting shape when the plant matures. Carries lilac-pink flowers and a fruity fragrance. Ideal for pots, so that it can then be moved under cover in winter.
**HABIT** Upright
↕ 2–4 ft (60 cm–1.2 m) ↔ initially 2–4 ft (60 cm–1.2 m); makes a 3–4 ft (90 cm–1.2 m) mound when mature
**COOK'S NOTES** Use young sprigs to flavor olive oil, or to infuse milk, cream, or syrup.

*Closely-packed leaves result in a bushy plant*

**ROSEMARY CORSICAN PROSTRATE'** ▶
*Rosmarinus officinalis* 'Corsican Prostrate'
❋ ☼

This variety has arching stems and deep blue flowers, and spreads by creeping roots.
**HABIT** Arching
↕ 12–18 in (30–45 cm) ↔ indefinite
**COOK'S NOTES** Good when in flower as a garnish for leg or rack of lamb.

**ROSEMARY 'MISS JESSOPP'S UPRIGHT'** ▶
*Rosmarinus officinalis* 'Miss Jessopp's Upright'
❋ ❋ ☼

Slender stems and excellent flavor for culinary uses. Place at the rear of the herb garden in a sunny spot.
**HABIT** Upright, bushy
↕ 4–6 ft (1.2–1.8 m)
↔ 30–36 in (75–90 cm)

*The blue flowers make an attractive garnish*

◀ **ROSEMARY 'TUSCAN BLUE'**
*Rosmarinus officinalis* 'Tuscan Blue'
❋ ❋ ☼

Very tall, slender, aromatic plant that eventually turns bare at the base. A more cold-hardy variety, but wrap stems in frost-prone areas.
**HABIT** Upright
↕ 6–7 ft (1.8–2.1 m) ↔ 12–24 in (30–60 cm)

# SAGE
*Salvia* spp.

This perennial herb family is huge, but most of its members are ornamental, apart from these key culinary ones. Its crinkled, musky leaves can be used fresh or dried.

**GROW** Sages like the warm, dry soils of their native Mediterranean. Sow seed or plant young plants in a part of the herb garden where you have dug sand into the soil for good drainage. Sage needs no special care but does require watering if the soil becomes too dry. Take cuttings in summer.

**HARVEST** Pick individual leaves as needed, or take whole stems for bouquet garni (see p128).

**COOK** Raw, fresh leaves are a little hairy and have a strong flavor, so chop them very finely and use in small amounts. Add toward the end of cooking to give a distinctive taste to risotto and pork, veal, and venison dishes; dried leaves are good for stuffings and with poultry, fish, potatoes, and carrots. You can use flowers to make summer teas.

*Variegated leaves in sage plants tend to have a milder flavor*

**GOLDEN SAGE ▶**
*Salvia officinalis* 'Icterina'
❀ ❀ ☼
Golden variegations of green leaves make this a great garnish. Boost its mild flavor by planting it in full sun.
**HABIT** Upright
↕ 24 in (60 cm) ↔ 24 in (60 cm)

*The leaves of this subtropical sage smell distinctly of pineapples*

## ▲PINEAPPLE SAGE ▲
*Salvia elegans* 'Scarlet Pineapple'
❀ ☼

This variety has slender, brittle stems with narrow, pineapple-scented leaves. It likes good, moist soil and may need support where growth is lush, and some frost protection.
**HABIT** Branching
‡ 3–4 ft (90 cm–1.2 m) ↔ 12–24 in (30–60 cm)
**COOK'S NOTES** Its scarlet flowers are good for salads.

## ▲ PURPLE SAGE
*Salvia officinalis* 'Purpurascens'
❀❀☼

Less potent than the common sage, but with an attractive spicy note in its flavor.
**HABIT** Low growing
‡ 12–18 in (30–45 cm)
↔ 18–24 in (45–60 cm)

## COMMON SAGE ▼
*Salvia officinalis*
❀❀☼

This is the best-known sage for culinary use. The oval leaves are highly aromatic and slightly spicy.
**HABIT** Low growing
‡ 12–18 in (30–45 cm)
↔ 24 in (60 cm)

## ◀THREE-COLOR SAGE
*Salvia officinalis* 'Tricolor'
❀❀☼

The leaf centers are green, but the margins run between pink and cream to striking effect. Full sun intensifies the color changes. It has a mild flavor.
**HABIT** Upright
‡ 12–24 in (30–60 cm) ↔ 24 in (60 cm)

# ELDER

*Sambucus* spp.

White flowers and small purple-black berries with a sweet muscat flavor are produced in profusion by this perennial. Both are used in cooking and for flavoring.

✿✿✿☼

**GROW** Sow seed in spring outdoors, or plant young plants in semi-shade and good, moist soil. Mulch with shredded leaves in fall. Take hardwood cuttings in fall.

**HARVEST** Pick flower heads in early summer and strip flowers off the stems. Harvest berries late in the season when they are purple-black. The berries are mildly poisonous when unripe and should not be eaten raw.

**COOK** Add flowers to drinks, cordials, custards, ice cream, and fruit desserts. Brew dried flowers for tisanes. Use berries in gelatin molds and for wine.

*Berries are mildly poisonous when raw*

## EUROPEAN ELDER (BLACK ELDER) ▼

*Sambucus nigra*

This variety is most commonly found in Europe, hence its common name. Plant where you need a windbreak or to screen an herb garden. Contact with the leaves may irritate skin.

**HABIT** Upright, shrubby
↕ 15–30 ft (4.5–6.1 m)
↔ 10–15 ft (3–4.5 m)

## ▲ AMERICAN ELDERBERRY

*Sambucus canadensis*

Grows wild in cold-winter areas of eastern North America. Prune to keep plants well behaved in the herb garden.

**HABIT** Shrubby, upright
↕ 10–12 ft (3–3.6 m) ↔ 10–12 ft (3–3.6 m)

*Do not eat the leaves, as they are purgative*

# SALAD BURNET
### *Sanguisorba minor*

This perennial is a pretty addition to an herb garden. Its toothed leaves are delicious in salads, imparting a cucumber-like taste.

❋ ❋ ❋ ☼ ◐

**GROW** Sow seed in spring in pots or in the garden. Salad burnet likes good garden soil and full sun to light shade. Pinch out flower buds and cut the leaves regularly to encourage new foliage.

**HARVEST** As it is an evergreen plant, you can clip leaves as needed year round.

**COOK** Add fresh leaves to mixed leaf salads.

**HABIT** Rosette forming
↕ 12 in (30 cm) ↔ 18–24 in (45–60 cm)

# STEVIA
### *Stevia rebaudiana*

The sugary tasting leaves of this perennial herb are 30–45 times sweeter than granulated sugar and have almost no calories.

❋ ❋ ❋ ☼

*The serrated leaves have a sugary flavor and a licorice aftertaste*

**GROW** Plant cuttings in acid soil in full sun in early summer. Sow seed indoors in late winter or early spring under cover and plant out when risk of frost has passed. Stevia requires a lot of water, so water deeply twice a week in the growing season.

**HARVEST** Pick individual leaves.

**COOK** Use the leaves fresh, dried, or ground, or boil them to make a syrup which can be used as a sugar substitute to sweeten desserts, fruit, and drinks.

**HABIT** Upright, bushy
↕ 18 in (45 cm) ↔ 18 in (45 cm)

# SAVORY
*Satureja* spp.

Plant both the perennial winter and annual summer savory in an herb garden and you can harvest their bitter, thyme-like leaves from spring until early winter.

**GROW** In spring, sow seed of both varieties in well-drained soil, or grow winter savory from cuttings. Enrich the soil with compost before planting and top-dress winter savory in pots.
**HARVEST** The leaves of summer savory have the most potency just before flowering. Winter savory is evergreen in all but very frosty regions, so it can be harvested any time.
**COOK** The fresh leaves of both varieties taste better young, but they keep their flavor when dried. Use sparingly in stuffings with other herbs. Good with veal and beans, peas, or other legumes.

*As it is evergreen, winter savory leaves can be harvested year-round*

**SUMMER SAVORY ▲**
*Satureja hortensis*
✹✹☼◐
This makes a good pot plant. Plant in partial shade in hot gardens.
**HABIT** Open, upright with trailing stems
↕ 18 in (45 cm) ↔ 18 in (45 cm)
**COOK'S NOTES** It is most often used in bean dishes.

**◀ WINTER SAVORY**
*Satureja montana*
✹✹✹☼
Plant this variety in full sun. It has a coarser, stronger flavor.
**HABIT** Dwarf, bushy
↕ 12–15 in (30–38 cm) ↔ about 24 in (60 cm)

# ALECOST
## *Tanacetum balsamita*

British brewers have flavored ales with this perennial herb since the Middle Ages. A few of its minty, sweet leaves go a long way in cooking.

**GROW** Sow seed indoors or divide roots and plant out in well-drained soil enriched with compost in a sunny spot. Give plants adequate water during the growing season. Cutting back stems to 9–12 in (22–30 cm) forces more pretty, scalloped basal leaves.

**HARVEST** Pick individual leaves from mid-summer into fall.

**COOK** Add fresh young leaves to salads, soups, stuffings, and cakes. Use leaves and flowers to make home-brewed beer.

**HABIT** Mat-forming, open
‡ 36 in (90 cm) ↔ 18 in (45 cm)

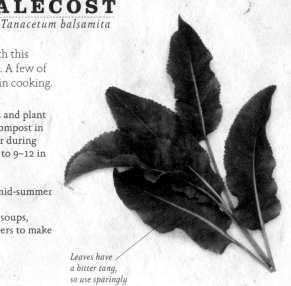

*Leaves have a bitter tang, so use sparingly*

# DANDELION
## *Taraxacum officinale*

This perennial plant needs no introduction. If it appears in your garden, harvest the leaves, for they make delicious bitter spring salad greens.

**GROW** This herb grows anywhere, but if it's not already in your garden, gather the seed from frothy seedheads in fields and lawns—but not too much. It needs no help to establish itself, other than a puff of breath to blow its seeds aloft. It will grow again from a tiny piece of root left in the soil.

**HARVEST** Gather the young leaves in early spring from your garden or places you know haven't been sprayed with herbicides or pesticides.

**COOK** Add fresh young leaves to salads, cook stems and larger leaves, which can be more bitter, and use petals in salads or to make wine.

**HABIT** Low-growing rosettes
‡ 12 in (30 cm) ↔ 18 in (45 cm)

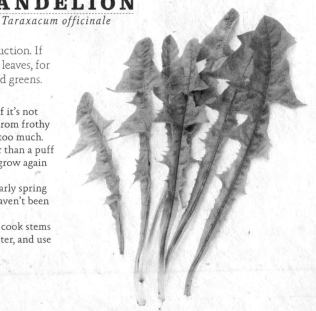

# THYME
*Thymus* spp.

An essential addition to any herb garden.
For a small plant, the leaves of this evergreen
perennial have a curiously strong flavor.
Bees love thyme's white to lilac flowers.

✸✸✸☼

**GROW** Sow seed in pots in spring (it may take
a month for them to germinate, so be patient) or
plant softwood cuttings. Thyme likes well-drained
sandy soil and doesn't require a lot of water. In very
hot climates, plant in semi-shade. Clumps can be
divided in late spring.

**HARVEST** Clip stems as you need them to keep
the plant from becoming woody and sparse.

**COOK** Add to any savory dish or use to make
bouquets garnis to flavor poultry, pork, and
fish dishes, or to add to stuffings and
vegetables. The leaves lose little of their flavor
when dried.

*A strong lemony flavor
makes this perfect
for cooking*

## ▲ CARAWAY THYME
*Thymus herba-barona*
The dark green leaves have a distinctive
caraway scent.
**HABIT** Low-growing, mat-forming
↕ 2–4 in (5–10 cm) ↔ 24 in (60 cm)
**COOK'S NOTES** Particularly good with
stir-fries and meat.

## ◄ LEMON THYME
*Thymus x citriodorus*
This is a very good thyme for
cooking, as the leaves have
a strong citrus aroma.
**HABIT** Upright
↕ 12 in (30 cm) ↔ 24 in (60 cm)
**COOK'S NOTES** Perfect partner
for chicken and fish dishes.

### ◀ ORANGE-SCENTED THYME

*Thymus* x *citriodorus* 'Fragrantissimus'

Use the spicy orange-scented leaves of this variety as a flavoring in place of orange peel.

**HABIT** Upright

‡ 12 in (30 cm) ↔ 8 in (20 cm)

*This bushy, sturdy plant produces stems with plenty of flavor-packed leaves*

### ▲ COMMON THYME

*Thymus vulgaris*

Give this variety a spot in full sun for the best flavor. It is the best-known thyme and the one most often used.

**HABIT** Compact, bushy

‡ 18 in (45 cm) ↔ 18 in (45 cm)

**COOK'S NOTES** Use in stews and casseroles.

### ▲ CONEHEAD THYME

*Thymus capitatus*

This thyme, which makes an aromatic tea, is the most widely used in the Middle East, where it's called *za-atar farsi* (Persian Thyme). It needs full sun and winter protection in cold regions.

**HABIT** Low-growing evergreen shrub

‡ 10 in (25 cm)

↔ 12 in (30 cm)

*Pretty grown in between stone steps, the aromatic leaves will withstand being trodden on*

### WILD CREEPING THYME ▶

*Thymus serpyllum*

A more mildly scented variety, but still good for culinary use and aesthetically a real joy to have in the garden.

**HABIT** Low-growing, mat-forming

‡ 1–3 in (2.5–7.5 cm)

↔ 36 in (90 cm)

# FENUGREEK
*Trigonella foenum-graecum*

Once used as animal fodder by the Greeks (its name means Greek hay), this annual herb has bitter leaves and maple-syrup-flavored seeds.

❀❀❀❀☼

**GROW** Sow seed in a sunny spot in good garden soil in late spring when the soil is thoroughly warm. It needs adequate water during the growing season.
**HARVEST** Pick leaves any time during the growing season. Collect seed pods when they ripen in the fall and dry them.
**COOK** Used by cooks in the Middle East and India, but less so in Europe or North America. Cook the bitter leaves in curries, use the seeds as a spice, and eat home-sprouted seeds in salads in small amounts.

**HABIT** Small, upright
‡ 24 in (60 cm) ↔ 12–18 in (30–45 cm)

*The leaves of fenugreek resemble those of clover*

# NASTURTIUM
*Tropaeolum majus*

This annual vine rambles over supports bearing yellow, orange, and red flowers. The leaves, seeds, and flowers all have a spicy, peppery taste.

❀❀❀☼

**GROW** Sow seed in spring in good, rich soil in a sunny spot where you have plenty of space. Water well during the hot summer months.
**HARVEST** Pick leaves and flowers to use fresh in summer, and pick the seed pods just before they turn from green to brown.
**COOK** Add the colorful flowers and the peppery leaves to salads, and the unripe seeds to sauces and dressings.

**HABIT** Climbing (bush types available)
‡ 6–8 ft (1.8–2.4 m) ↔ 12 in (30 cm)

# ENGLISH VIOLET
## *Viola odorata*

The sweetly scented flowers of this perennial have long been used in perfumes and cookery. The leaves and flowers taste of Parma violets.

❀❀❀💧☀☀

**GROW** Violets are natural denizens of woodlands and shady areas but will tolerate full sun in cool climates. Sow seed or bulblets in a suitable spot in your garden and they will spread themselves with abandon. Snip off tops after the frosts, then fertilize with a top dressing of compost early in the spring.

**HARVEST** Pick the little fragrant violet flowers as they appear. Harvest the milder-tasting leaves throughout the summer, as needed.

**COOK** Use the flowers in salads, to flavor drinks, as a coloring agent, and once crystallized, to decorate desserts. Add the leaves to salads.

**HABIT** Low-growing, clump-forming
↕ 6 in (15 cm) ↔ 12 in (30 cm)

*Pretty purple flowers make a delicate garnish*

*A few leaves are palatable, but too many can cause digestive upset*

# GINGER
## *Zingiber officinale*

This ancient perennial herb is a tropical one, but the edible roots can be successfully grown under cover in a temperate climate.

❀ ☀

**GROW** Buy cuttings or fresh roots in early spring and break them into 2-in (5-cm) pieces. Let the ends dry, then plant them just below the surface of a rich, moist soil. Ginger likes heat and humidity, so grow it in a pot that you can bring indoors in winter.

**HARVEST** After 3 months, dig up the plants. Discard the leaves and store the roots in a moist paper towel in the salad drawer of the fridge for up to 3 weeks. It freezes well.

**COOK** Grate the root to add a refreshing tang to stir-fries, curries, cookies, cakes, desserts, chocolate, and teas. Use frozen roots straight from the freezer.

**HABIT** Upright
↕ 5 ft (1.5 m) ↔ indefinite

*Beneath delicate aromatic leaves lies a deliciously spicy edible root*

# GROW

Once you've chosen your herbs, it's time to
get growing. Find out how and where you
can sow seed or grow young plants, how
to keep them fed, watered, healthy, and
productive throughout the growing season,
and how to create new plants from old.

# CLIMATE

Try to choose perennials that will thrive in your local climate. The symbols here (and in The Herb Catalog) show a plant's ability to survive cold and wet climates and indicate, therefore, which conditions best enable these perennials to return each spring, or if herbs must be grown from seed each year.

## ❄ ❄ ❄ HARDY HERBS

These herbs can stay outside over winter in regions where temperatures drop to a minimum of 5°F (-15°C) and the ground freezes solid, as they are adapted to survive in these conditions.
Five such plants are illustrated here.

Roman chamomile
*Chamaemelum nobile*

Chives
*Allium schoenoprasum*

Mints
*Mentha* spp.

Thymes
*Thymus* spp.

Lemon balm
*Melissa officinalis*

## ❄❄ FROST-HARDY HERBS

Where winter minimums do not fall below 23°F (-5°C), climates can be warm and dry (typically similar to that of the Mediterranean, with dry summers and wet winters), or warm and moist. In these regions you can grow most of the hardy and frost-hardy herbs (such as those pictured here), as well as more tender perennials that might not survive the winter in colder areas. If temperatures are forecast to drop below this minimum, some of these plants may need some protection if they are to survive, undamaged, until spring.

Common sage
*Salvia officinalis*

Arugula
*Eruca vesicaria*
subsp. *sativa*

Dittany of Crete
oregano
*Origanum
dictamnus*

Bay leaf
*Laurus nobilis*

Rosemary
*Rosmarinus
officinalis*

# ❄ HALF-HARDY HERBS

These herbs can be killed by frosts and severe winter weather, but they flourish where temperatures do not drop below 32°F (0°C). Do not plant in frost pockets (areas where cold air and frost collect). If frost is forecast, protect plants such as those shown below with mulch, cover with cloches or insulating fleece, or bring them indoors into a sunny spot.

Curry leaf
*Murraya koenigi*

Sweet
marjoram
*Origanum
majorana*

Chilli
peppers
*Capsicum*
spp.

Scented
geranium
*Pelargonium*
spp.

French
lavender
*Lavandula
dentata*

## ⬦ HERBS TOLERANT OF WET SOILS

Not many herbs like getting their feet wet, but there
are a few (including those pictured here) that will tolerate
moist but well-drained soils. If you have a spot with
constantly wet soil, try some of
these herbs. All will do well in
dappled shade, too.

Mints
*Mentha* spp.

Bergamot
*Monarda
didyma*

English
violet
*Viola
odorata*

Watercress
*Nasturtium
officinale*

Meadowsweet
*Filipendula ulmaria*

# PLANNING

Once you've identified your climate, it's time to choose where—or in what—to grow your herbs. Do you want to grow just a few herbs in pots, or would you like a more elaborate plot? Be mindful of how much sun your herbs need and position them appropriately in your garden.

**Oregano** *This herb will thrive in a pot and can easily be moved to a sheltered spot over winter.*

### POTS

Most culinary herbs take well to pot culture. Container growing can produce good results, as you can move plants around the garden to get the most sun or to give them some shade on very sunny days. It is also easier to move frost-tender plants indoors into a sunny spot during winter months. However, plants in pots also require frequent watering—daily in the summer. If you have a south-facing fence or wall, dress it up with a window box or wall-mounted pots spilling over with greenery. Window boxes allow you to grow a good selection of herbs in one space, and can be conveniently positioned by a kitchen window to make picking for cooking even easier. Plant herbs in generous containers with drainage holes in the bottom. Use fine soil mixed in equal quantities with vermiculite for the Mediterranean herbs, and 100 percent potting soil for delicate herbs such as chervil or French tarragon.

### INVASIVE HERBS

Some herbs can be invasive and take over the herb garden if left unchecked, so these are good candidates for planting in pots. These include:

• Mints *Mentha* spp.
• Bergamot *Monarda didyma*
• Lemon balm *Melissa officinalis*
• Mustard *Brassica* spp.
• Purslane *Portulaca oleracea*
• Lovage *Levisticum officinale*

**Use your space** *Position pots against a south-facing wall in a sheltered spot to give them the best of the sun.*

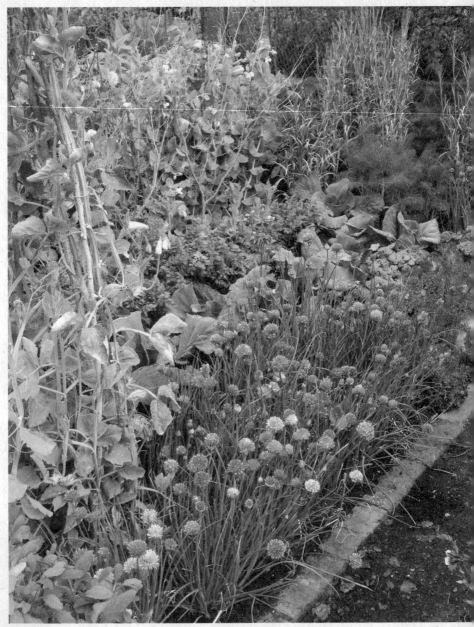

**Sharing space** Chives and other herbs make pretty and practical additions to vegetable beds.

## BEDS AND BORDERS

If you have already laid out a vegetable garden, or ornamental beds or borders, plant your culinary herbs between the plants that are already there. Position sun-loving herbs where they'll get lots of light, and tuck shade-lovers around taller ornamentals.

A small, informal, dedicated, culinary herb garden might occupy as little as 5 x 12 ft (1.5 x 3.5 m), but you can still pack in plenty of herbs. You do not need a path, as you will easily be able to reach all the plants from either side. If you have a choice as to where to put the herb garden, position it where you can see it best. It could also be planted within a larger vegetable garden.

A formal arrangement is possible even in the tiniest garden. In an ornamental herb garden or kitchen garden, you could plant low-growing herbs, such as Mother of Thyme or chamomile, between paths made of crushed rock, bricks, or flagstones.

Sketch out your dream garden on graph paper before you dig it. Then mark out planting areas in geometric or soft, curving patterns. If you add trellises, arbors, arches, pillars, water features, and statues you can give it a formal look. If you have a sloping garden, terraces make a beautiful addition.

## PICK PLANTS FOR PLACES

No matter how tolerant a plant, there are some spots in the garden where plants simply don't thrive, so avoid panting anything there. Large trees and big, woody shrubs, for instance, commandeer all the available water and nutrients in their root zones.

Slopes drain quickly and are not suitable for moisture-loving herbs such as mints, but are an ideal place for drought-tolerant herbs such as lavender and rosemary. Low areas that remain constantly wet will rot the roots of all but bog-loving plants such as meadowsweet.

Beware of frost pockets (see p78) for plants that feel the cold—these will kill or shorten the growing season of less hardy herbs.

## PLANT PARTNERS

Your herb garden will look its best when you match plants by following one simple rule: contrast. This works well both in the herb garden and when planting herbs within vegetable beds or ornamental borders.

Plant plants with small leaves, such as chervil or cilantro next to plants with large leaves, such as horseradish or even rhubarb. Juxtapose colored leaves of red perilla and purple basil with green- or gray-leaved plants. Contrast the architecture of tall, thin plants such as fennel with low-growing mounds of lemon balm. You do not have to restrict yourself to herbs; add color and excitement by interplanting flowers such as annual marigolds, ranunculus, petunias, and zinnias; or dramatic perennials such as perovskia and kniphofia.

Some woody herbs, such as bay leaf and rosemary, can be trained as standards with a 2–3-ft (60–90-cm) stem and a ball of leaves on top. Standards are usually grown in generous pots that can be moved around the garden or patio to catch the sun. They look attractive when underplanted with low-growing herbs or annual flowers.

*Bay leaf tree*
*Underplant standards, such as bay leaf, with other herbs to create a decorative display.*

# SOIL

In pots, it is easy to control the soil you use, but when planting into the garden you need to check your soil type. Garden soils are mostly loam, sandy, or clay. The best is loam, which is a combination of clay and sand. Clay is wet and heavy and needs compost and sand added to improve aeration; sandy soil is dry and light, and is only able to retain water and nutrients when you add compost to it.

## TESTING SOIL

Try this simple test to discover the composition of your soil before planting your herb garden.

**1** Take samples from three spots in the area where you want to grow herbs. Using a hand fork, remove any grass, weeds, or plants from the surface of the soil.

**2** Push your spade down as deep as the blade will go and lift out a clod of earth. Repeat in two other places in your herb-garden patch.

**3** Place the samples together in a paper bag and mix thoroughly, crumbling any clumps with your fingers. Discard any rocks that are larger than pea-sized.

**4** Squeeze some soil in your palm and thump it with a finger. If it falls apart, it is loam; if it is gritty, it is sandy; if it forms a lump, as pictured, you have clay.

# MAKING COMPOST

You can save yourself the expense of buying compost by making your own. Simply layer grass clippings, leaves, uncooked vegetable waste, and dead (but not diseased) plants into a compost bin that is 5 ft (1.5 m) square and 3 ft (90 cm) high. Do not add weeds or grass that have set seed. Farm-animal manure is an excellent addition—use one-sixth manure to one-part plant matter.

**1** Collect your compostable material in a bin. Keep the heap moist and turn it every two weeks, using a fork or shovel, until the ingredients start to break down.

**2** You can use your compost when it has turned dark brown in color, is crumbling in texture, and looks and smells like soil.

### pH LEVEL

Some herbs, such as angelica, prefer soil that is slightly acidic while others, such as thyme, favor alkaline soil, so it is a good idea to determine your soil's pH level. The pH level affects how plants get hold of the nutrients they need; most soil nutrients are available to plants in slightly acidic soils, about pH 6.8, but at either end of the scale nutrients become chemically locked up and unavailable. You can buy a simple test from your garden center, then take a soil sample and add it to a test tube with the supplied solution. The indicator paper will reveal the pH of your soil.

# GROWING FROM SEED

There are many advantages to growing herbs from seed. Home-sown herbs are cheaper than those bought from a nursery, and home-grown seedlings have healthy, garden-ready root balls when the time comes to plant them out. Some herbs are best propagated in other ways, though (see pp90–1).

Some seeds are too small to be scarified using a knife or piece of sandpaper, so in this case use the edge of a nail file instead.

## SCARIFYING SEED

If you are growing from seed, bear in mind that they all have different germination requirements; some may benefit from an overnight soak in water before planting in pots or in the garden, such as parsley, and a very few may need scarifying—a technique whereby you nick seeds with a knife or a piece of rough sandpaper to allow air and moisture in. Plants that need scarifying are those such as bay and cilantro, that have hard hulls. Always follow the instructions on the seed packets for the individual cultivation requirements of the herbs and directions for sowing.

## SOWING THE SEED

Sow seed into a plastic tray, a cellular tray, or into individual plastic or terra-cotta pots. Tap-rooted herbs do not like to be transplanted, so sow them in peat pots that can be planted out, pot and all.

**I** Fill a pot with fine soil and gently firm it down. Water the soil and let it drain. Sow seed in dents or on the soil surface (according to the packet instructions).

**2** Lightly cover the seed with vermiculite or more potting soil. Water again. Set the tray in a warm place and never let the soil dry out.

# TRANSPLANTING

As seedlings develop they need more space to grow. Transplant them into individual or bigger pots (about 6-in (15-cm) pots are big enough, or go one size up from the pot they are already in), when they have formed four or more true leaves above the seed leaves.

## HARDEN OFF

When all risk of frost is past, start to acclimatize, or harden off, transplanted plants to outdoor temperatures. Put seedlings outside during the day, uncovered, and bring them in at night. After a week you can plant them or leave them out.

**I** Remove the seedlings carefully from their container, gently pulling them out by holding the true leaves, not the stem, while lightly squeezing the bottom of the pot.

**2** Make a hole with your finger in a pot of fresh soil to the depth of the seedling's root ball, then gently lower in the seedling to the same level as it was planted before.

**3** Once the seedling is in position, backfill around the root ball of the plant with more soil and gently firm it down around the roots.

**4** Water the plant well, label it, and position it in a warm, bright spot out of direct sunlight until it is mature enough to plant into its final position.

# GROWING YOUNG PLANTS

Sometimes it may not be practical to raise plants from seed yourself, especially if you only want to grow a handful of different plants and don't have space to sow lots of seedlings, or if a plant is hard to grow from seed. Garden centers have a good selection, but nurseries have a broader range.

## PICK A PERFECT PLANT

Do not buy plants with obvious problems or diseases, such as leaves with yellow veins or mildew. Herbs should have bright, sturdy stems and foliage, but knock the plant out of its pot and check the roots too; they should be healthy and plentiful and not fighting for space (see below). Check plants for live insects; you do not want to bring a problem home.

*Leaves should have a good, healthy color*

*Soil should be moist and free of weeds*

*Plants should have sturdy stems*

*Check the roots for pest damage and to see if they are potbound*

## GET TO THE ROOT OF THE PROBLEM

Vigorous leaves and stems do not always mean the plant is disease free; sometimes problems lie beneath the soil. Roots are the lifeline of plants, so it is important that they are healthy.

**GOOD** The plant should easily lift out of its pot and the roots should be plentiful but not overcrowded, with plenty of soil visible.

**BAD** Tease out and thin overcrowded roots before planting out in good soil. Check for root weevils and grubs.

## POTTING ON

If you want to grow your herb in a pot, replant when you get it home in a pot one size bigger than it is in. You will need to repeat the process when your plants outgrow their new pots.

**1** Make sure the new pot has a drainage hole, and place a handful of gravel in the bottom. Half-fill with potting compost and remove the plant from its pot.

**2** Set the plant in the new pot and fill the space around the root ball with potting soil, firming it in gently as you go. Water the plant well.

## PLANTING INTO THE GARDEN

Young plants bought from a nursery should be big enough to plant outdoors in the garden immediately. Plant them out as soon as you can to allow their roots to establish.

**1** Prepare the soil by digging into the top 6–12 in (15–30 cm) of soil until the soil becomes loose and friable. Dig a generous hole in the prepared soil.

**2** Place the plant in the hole to the depth it was in its pot. Backfill with soil around the plant and firm it in with the palms of your hands. Water the plant well.

# PROPAGATING

Once plants are established, you can increase their number, or grow insurance plants in case some do not survive winter, by various propagating methods. See the individual entries in The Herb Catalog for the best technique to use.

## STEM CUTTINGS

You can take cuttings from stems at different times of the year. Take softwood cuttings from young, flexible stems in spring, semi-ripe ones from ripening, stiffening stems in late summer, and hardwood ones from stems that are turning woody at the end of the growing season.

1 Select a healthy, non-flowering stem with mature leaves, such as this rosemary. Cut the stem at an angle just above the leaf attachment. Strip the lower leaves.

2 Cut the stem straight across, 2 in (5 cm) below the last leaf. Plant vertically in a pot of soil. Water well. Cover the pot with a clear plastic bag to retain moisture.

## ROOT CUTTINGS

Make new plants from sections of semi-mature or mature roots of plants, such as mints and sweet cicely, when they are dormant (not growing), in mid- to late winter. Watercress is one exception to this rule, as root cuttings can be taken from it all year round.

1 Lift the plant and tease the roots apart a little to find some good roots to use as cuttings—do not use any that are fibrous and immature.

2 Cut a 2-in (5-cm) piece; trim it straight across at the top and make a sloping cut at the base. Plant cuttings vertically in soil and cover with vermiculite.

## LAYERING
This is a good method for propagating woody plants while stems are still attached to the plant.

**1** In the dormant season, remove leaves from 4–20 in (10–50 cm) behind the tip of a flexible stem.

**2** Add soil and sand where you will bury the stem. Peg the bent stem down toward the soil.

**3** Cover the stem with soil, allowing the tip to protrude. Water well. In the fall, detach and pot up the plant.

## DIVIDING PERENNIALS
Every three or four years, or when plants become too large, divide perennial herbs such as fennel.

**1** Lift the entire plant using a garden fork and wash the soil off the root ball with a hose.

**2** Take sections from the perimeter of the root ball, separating them by hand or with a sturdy knife.

**3** Replant the crowns in good garden soil and water in well. Discard the woody central clump.

## DIVIDING BULBS
Bulbous plants, such as garlic, produce bulblets which you can detach to create new plants.

**1** Lift bulbs in the fall when the top growth has yellowed. Separate the bulblets around the base of the bulb.

**2** Replant the bulblets in pots of fresh, moist soil to a depth of twice their length.

**3** Cover the bulblets with fresh soil and water well. Grow until well established, then plant out.

# FEEDING AND WATERING

Herbs grown in pots and those grown in the ground have different requirements. The individual entries in The Herb Catalog list specific wants and needs, but these general guidelines will keep all plants healthy.

## WATERING HERBS IN BEDS

If you are planting a selection of herbs in the garden you cannot always cater for individual preferences, but plants will usually tolerate shared conditions, as long as they have moist, well-drained soil. Work lots of compost into the soil to help it retain moisture and water it deeply when the top 2 in (5 cm) seems dry. The best time to water, if you are using an overhead sprinkler or watering can, is in the morning, so the sun has time to dry the leaves. Plants are most vulnerable to mildew and rot when they are wet during the night.

*Water early* Try to water your herbs in the morning.

## FEEDING HERBS IN BEDS

Plants in open ground do not need much feeding because their roots travel to find the nutrition they require. However, you can give them a helping hand by spreading a 2-in (5-cm) layer of compost over the soil surface as a mulch over winter, then by digging it into the soil in spring to restore nutrients. Herbs that are harvested frequently during the growing season benefit from the occasional fertilizer feed in mid-summer too.

*Homemade compost* makes a good mulch

In a watering can, add granular or liquid fertilizer to water to feed herbs during the growing season. Follow the application instructions on the packet.

## WATERING HERBS IN POTS

Plants in pots need to be watered more often than those in the ground, as their roots cannot travel as far to locate moisture. In hot summers you should water them every day, or install drip irrigation systems in each pot and set timers to automatically water them. You can help the soil to retain more water using special granules that absorb water and release it as and when needed.

Pour some potting soil onto a flat surface and add a handful of the moisture-retaining granules.

2 Work the granules into the soil with your fingers so they are evenly mixed.

3 Half-fill the pot with the soil mix before planting your herb, then top up with more soil.

## FEEDING HERBS IN POTS

Potted plants also need more attention than those in the ground when it comes to food. Ideally, you should feed potted herbs with fertilizer in granules or liquid form every 6 weeks throughout the growing season, especially if they are being regularly harvested.

Start feeding in spring when plants begin to produce new growth. It is also beneficial to scrape away the top 2 in (5 cm) of soil in the pot in spring and replace it with good, fresh soil. Stop feeding them in late summer, or you will encourage new growth when the plant should be slowing down before the dormant winter season.

Feed potted herbs with fertilizer in granules or in liquid form every 6 weeks during the growing season.

# WEED CONTROL

Weeds compete with plants for water, sunlight, nutrients, and space, and if allowed to grow freely they will overwhelm the garden. The key to defeating weeds is to remove them as you see them. Make sure you remove all parts of them, including the root, to prevent regrowth.

### BEATING WEEDS

Once the weeds start to appear in spring, you need to remove them by hand or with the help of a hand-fork where they have long roots. To help prevent them returning, remove weeds before they set seed and make sure you get as much of the root out of the soil as possible, particularly with perennial weeds. Check the soil regularly for any new shoots appearing and remove them immediately. If you want to clear a large area of weeds before planting in it, try either solarizing (see below) or using a mulch (see opposite).

**Weeding by hand** *This is the most effective way of removing all parts of weeds once they are established.*

### SOLARIZING

This is a good method for clearing both small and large sections of soil of weeds. It is a chemical-free technique, which kills weeds, bacteria, and nematodes in the soil before you plant.

In early summer, clear a patch of soil of any plants, weeds, or large stones, and level it off. Water it thoroughly until it is soaked, then cover the area with clear plastic sheeting and bury it at the edges to prevent air getting in or out. (Do not use black or colored sheeting because they block the sun's rays; transparent sheeting allows the rays to penetrate and turn into sterilizing heat.) Over the next 6–8 weeks, the sun will create killing heat and steam under the plastic. After that time, remove the plastic and plant the herbs immediately, trying to disturb the soil as little as possible. Mulch the patch once you have planted out the herbs.

## MULCHES

Laying down a 6-in (15-cm) mulch in spring just as new growth emerges will stop weed germination, but as it rots down the soil nitrogen level will deplete, so spread a 2-in (5-cm) layer of compost on the soil before mulching. Top with a mulch of your choice—it can be purely practical or more aesthetically pleasing. Pull up any weeds that find their way through the mulch.

Lay thick sections of newspaper on the soil above the plant's roots, leaving only a small space around the stem. Hold the paper down with stones.

Chipped or shredded bark makes a good mulch in its own right, or can be used to cover other less attractive mulches such newspaper or weed-suppressant matting.

For a neat and tidy mulch, place a 6–8-in (15–20-cm) layer of weed-seed-free compost on the soil and cover it with a good layer of gravel.

Weed-seed-free hay makes an attractive, effective, and nutritious mulch that will improve the soil and feed plants as it decays.

# IMPROVING YOUR HARVEST

To keep the garden tidy and productive, some maintenance is required at different times of the year. A little pruning and deadheading goes a long way toward increasing your plants' productivity and ensuring that the harvest keeps coming, sometimes even into the winter months.

## THE GROWING SEASON

Spring and summer are the times of year when growth is fastest, so maintenance during this growing season means more than just keeping the soil moist and pulling up weeds. You need to remove flowers from herbs whose leaves are used in cooking, as this forces the plants' energies into making new, leafy growth. Both perennial and annual herbs have a growth cycle that tends to shut down once it produces seed, so deadhead flowers and remove flower stalks to prevent plants going to seed. Keep an eye out for pests or diseases (see pp98–101), and for animal damage. If some stalks, stems, or leaves are yellowing, clip them off, as well as any dead or diseased tissue. If an herb is outgrowing its spot or crowding other useful plants, trim it back. Tie in climbing stems to trellis or supports as they appear.

## REMOVE FLOWERS

Cut off flowers as they open during the growing season; it also promotes new blooms.

## PINCHING OUT

Removing the growing tips and developing flower buds encourages more leafy growth.

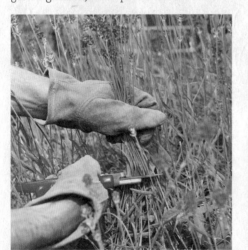

Using a pair of sharp, clean pruning shears, cut back lavender and other flowering herbs after harvesting their blooms. Trim them to a neat shape.

Using your thumb and forefinger, remove any developing flower buds or growing tips on herbs that you are growing for their leaves only.

## CUT BACK OLD GROWTH

As the weather turns cold in fall and winter, cut back any dying, yellowing growth. In early spring, hard prune perennial herbs such as lavender to encourage new growth and a neat shape.

Using pruning shears, prune back old, dead wood to the point at which the plant is starting to regrow, such as where you can see new buds forming.

**2** Leave 1–2 in (2.5–5 cm) of last season's growth and add a thick mulch to protect frost-tender plants from winter weather, if necessary.

## CONTAINER CARE

Plants growing in containers have restricted space and a limited amount of soil, so these herbs do need special care. As well as supplementary feeding (see p93), add fresh compost to the pot halfway through the growing season to boost the soil's nutrient level, and water regularly throughout the growing season; daily in hot temperatures. Pot-grown plants benefit from repotting every now and again. So, every spring, check to see if potted plants have become root-bound, and if they have, repot them into new containers (see p88–9). However, if repotting isn't practical, just remove the plant from its pot, loosen tangled roots and prune back the root ball a little, remove 1 in (2.5 cm) of surface soil, then return it to its pot. Top up to just below the rim with fresh compost or good potting soil.

Herbs in containers benefit from constant harvesting to encourage new growth and to keep the plants under control in their restricted space.

# PESTS

One of the virtues of many culinary herbs—especially Mediterranean herbs—is that the aromatic volatile oils they exude are produced primarily to ward off insects. So, many of the plants in your herb garden will naturally protect themselves against pests. However, here are a few pests to look out for.

## LEAF MINERS

Tiny worms will bore through the tissues inside leaves, causing clearly visible, twisting white trails. The best control is to pick off and destroy infested leaves when you see them.

## CATERPILLARS

Chewed leaves are the work of many pests but caterpillars are some of the worst offenders. Pick them off by hand several times weekly (wear a glove, as some have spines that can irritate skin), and dispose of them as you wish. You can also encourage native parasitic wasps to feast on them by planting flowering herbs that attract them, such as dill or sweet woodruff, or spray infested plants with a special homemade solution. (Blend a peeled head of garlic with two cups of water and strain the liquid before use.)

*Slugs Pillagers of young plants and fresh growth.*

## SLUGS AND SNAILS

The bane of all gardeners' lives, slugs and snails chew on young seedlings or new fresh growth and leave little to crop. There are many theories about how best to control them. If you are an organic gardener you can use slug traps—these are pots that have a little beer in the bottom and which are sunk into the soil alongside prized or particularly vulnerable plants. The snails and slugs are lured to the traps by the smell, fall in, and then drown. You need to empty the pots of dead creatures regularly and refill with beer. Alternatively, you can pick the slugs and snails off plants by hand, if you are prepared to venture out at night to do this, when they are most active. Again, the best control is to drown the insects; do not throw them over the fence, as they have a tendency to return. If you don't want to get this close to them, you could try the non-toxic, organic pellets that are available.

### SHORT, SHARP SHOCK

Apply copper tape just below the rim of pots or other containers to deter slugs and snails. This metallic tape gives them a mild electrical shock as they pass over it.

## ROSEMARY BEETLES

Distinctive colorful markings make rosemary beetles easy to identify. They eat the leaves and tips of lavender, rosemary, sage, and thyme, causing serious damage. Pick them off by hand and destroy them as you see them.

## VINE WEEVILS

A major pest, these grubs come out at night, mostly in spring and fall, and chew notches out of leaf margins and devour roots. They are difficult to control biologically, but you can add nematodes to the soil to kill them.

**Beautiful but deadly** Rosemary beetles destroy herbs.

**Night terrors** Nocturnal leaf- and root-eating grubs.

## APHIDS

These plant-sucking pests, along with scale, whitefly, mealy bugs, thrips, spittle bugs, and red spider mites, will weaken a plant's growth. Spritz them off plants as you see them with a forceful jet of water from a hose, or use an organic, insecticidal soap.

## BAY SUCKER NYMPHS

If the edges of the leaves on your bay leaf plant suddenly start to thicken, yellow, and curl, it may be suffering an infestation of this sap-sucking insect. Pick off the greenish-brown, winged adults as you see them and remove and destroy any affected leaves.

**Tiny suckers** Aphids drain the life from healthy herbs.

**Greedy nymphs** These cause leaves to thicken and curl.

# DISEASES

Most herbs are remarkably free of plant diseases, and many can be prevented by good care and maintenance when working among your plants, but occasionally diseases do develop. If you deal with them quickly, though, you can avoid any lasting damage to the plant.

## AVOID DISEASES

Herbs are seldom attacked by bacterial and fungal diseases, and often prevention is the best cure. There are several ways in which you can protect your herbs. Grow resistant varieties and apply good cultural practices and hygiene in the garden. Do not feed plants as the fall's cool weather sets in, as this stimulates weak growth. Try not to work in the garden when it is wet as you may inadvertently spread diseases. Sterilize your clippers between each cut, even while pruning healthy plants, to prevent any latent diseases spreading or developing. Dip the blades into a solution that is 10 percent bleach and 90 percent water, then carefully wipe them dry using a clean cloth. Examine plants regularly and act quickly if you spot signs of disease. Remove infected leaves as they fall and do not leave them lying on the soil surface. Make sure that you dispose of any infected plant material carefully—preferably by burning it. Do not place infected material on the compost heap.

*Keep clippers clean* Sterilize them to prevent spreading infections around the herb garden.

## BACTERIA

Sometimes bacteria will enter the plant through wounds. If this happens you can treat the plant with a commercial spray or make your own organic version. Spray the affected plants with a mixture made from a dozen garlic cloves puréed in 2.5 pints (1.2 liters) of water and strained. If the plants do not respond within days, clip off and destroy the infected parts. Remember to sterilize your clippers before you use them again.

*Sprays* Use an organic spray to treat any bacterial diseases that affect your plants.

## FUNGI

This type of disease is fairly rare among herbs, although mint is prone to rust, and downy and powdery mildews can develop in humid, warm, and wet climatic conditions. There are organic controls for fungal diseases. Fungus prefers a slightly acid leaf surface, so spraying with an alkaline solution can prevent it taking hold. Spray with elemental sulfur, or Bordeaux mixture, or make your own solution. Mix 1 heaped tbsp of baking soda with 1 tbsp of dormant oil (available at garden centers), ½ tsp of insecticidal soap (or dishwashing liquid), in 1 gallon (4 liters) of lukewarm water. Spray when plants are young or seedlings show four true leaves. Reapply after rain. Do not use more than the recommended amount of baking soda, as too much can defoliate plants.

**Powdery mildew** *A white fungus develops on leaves.*

## VIRUSES

The varied symptoms of viral diseases make them difficult to identify. Among the most common are mosaic viruses, which cause white, yellow, or light green dots on leaves. Viruses often cause curled leaves, too, and ring spot viruses result in pale, yellowed ringed spots on leaves. Viruses do not cause any serious damage, but if you wish, pull up affected plants and destroy them.

**Curled leaves** *This can be a sign of a virus that has been transmitted by sucking insects or infected tools.*

**Rust** *Unsightly small brown patches of spores appear on the underside of leaves.*

# HARVEST
# AND STORE

There are a few golden rules to follow to ensure you go on harvesting your herbs for months. Besides cutting to use fresh, harvest the leaves, flowers, seedheads, and roots to store for use when fresh herbs are not available after the growing season.

# REAPING THE HARVEST

Herbs contain myriad culinary components. Besides the leaves, you can use the stalks, stems, flowers, seeds, berries, and even the root. At the end of the growing season, harvest and dry the whole plant to use throughout the winter.

## HOW AND WHEN TO PICK

Harvesting various parts of herbs involves different techniques and timings to ensure you pick them when they are full of flavor. You can cut herbs for using fresh throughout the growing season, and even through the winter if they are evergreen. However, if you want to harvest leafy herbs for drying or to store, pick them in early summer when they have the most flavor—just before the flower buds open. Herbs produce their flavorsome volatile oils at night because the hot midday sun evaporates them each day, so the best time to harvest is in the early morning. Flowers appear from spring through summer and can be picked for use as they appear, but if you want the seeds for cooking, or for sowing the next year, leave the flower heads untrimmed. They will then set seed, ready to be cut down, dried, and stored in the fall.

*Keep picking Harvest little and often to encourage new fresh growth*

### DO'S

• Snip off stems and leaves early in the day, before the sun is at its strongest.

• Always use a sharp, clean knife or pair of clippers or scissors.

• Harvest from all over the plant to keep it neat.

• Feed herbs with liquid fertilizer after making a substantial harvest.

### DON'TS

• Avoid cutting into old, woody growth, as it may not re-grow.

• Do not use leaves and flowers that are damaged or discolored; remove and discard them.

• Do not deadhead flowers on the plant in late summer if you want to collect seeds in the fall.

• Do not scrub leaves vigorously—rinse and pat dry.

## LEAVES

Leaves are the most commonly used part of herbs. Take leaves from here and there all over the plant rather than from one spot so the plant keeps a neat, balanced shape.

Pinch off the tender sage leaves with their stalks at the tips of their stems, either using scissors, clippers, or your thumb and forefinger.

## STALKS

Technically these are the stems of a leaf, but sometimes, as with chives, they are also the leaf itself. Never cut off chives completely. This exhausts and damages the bulbs.

*Chive spears* Take individual spears from here and there

## STEMS

The stems are the main axis of the plant, supporting leaves and flowers. In clump-forming herbs, cut the stems 1 in (2.5 cm) above the soil level to enable them to regrow.

*Take stems* Harvest stems of rosemary and strip off the leaves between thumb and forefinger (see p122)

*Keep it neat* Cut individual lavender stems to keep the plant's shape

## FLOWERS

Cut off stems of small flowers such as lavender and meadowsweet using clippers, or pick large blooms such as marigold by hand.

If you want only a few individual flowers, such as nasturtiums, pick them off the plant using your thumb and forefinger, taking as little stalk as possible.

## SEEDS

Harvest seeds from anise, fennel, caraway (here), and cilantro while still on the plant, or cut off stems with seedheads to dry (see p116).

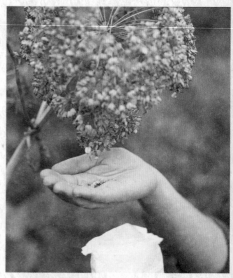

Put a sheet underneath the plant from which you want to harvest seeds, then gently shake the seedheads over your hand. What you don't catch, the sheet will.

## BERRIES

Most berries are ripe if they come away from the plants easily when gently tugged. Black currants and elderberries can be carefully stripped from the stems using your fingers, or you can snip off the complete trusses and separate the berries from the stems back in the kitchen.

To harvest ripe black currants, hold the stem between two fingers and run them down the length to strip off the berries into the palm of your other hand.

## ROOTS

If harvesting during the growing season, expose roots of plants such as ginger and horseradish with a trowel, then cut portions of root from the mother plant with pruners or the sharp edge of a spade before replanting the roots. If you are lifting the whole plant in the fall to keep it indoors over the winter, wash off the soil and remove the stems, then leave to dry off. Lay the whole, dry roots on sand in trays, cover with more sand, and store in a cool, dark place, such as a garage.

Using a trowel, carefully dig out the roots of the horseradish plant and lift them onto the soil surface, taking care not to damage them.

## WHOLE PLANT

If you are using more than one section of a plant at a time, or you are cutting down plants at the end of the growing season to store, remove individual stems or flower stalks of clump-forming herbs such as lovage, angelica, fennel, lavender, lemongrass, salad burnet, and watercress. If it is during the growing season, do not take more than half the plant to allow it to regrow. Cut the stems just above the soil level. If you want the root, too, dig up the whole plant and harvest the parts individually.

To harvest complete stems from a plant, cut them off about 2 in (5 cm) above the soil level using clippers.

# SHORT-TERM STORAGE

Herbs are at their most fragrant and vibrantly flavorful straight from the garden. It's always best to pick what you need for a dish or a meal and use it immediately, but that may not always be convenient. However, there are a number of techniques that help keep herbs as "garden fresh" as possible. For use within hours of harvesting, keep them handy on the worktop. For use within a few days, prepare the herbs ahead and chill them.

*__On the worktop__ Delicate herbs such as tarragon, parsley, chervil, mint, oregano, or cilantro keep well for a few days in a jug or vase of fresh water.*

## CHOPPED HERBS IN THE FRIDGE

Preparing chopped herbs ahead saves you time at the last minute. This is useful when you need a lot of fresh herbs, such as chives, mint, or basil, for several dishes, or you are cooking for a crowd.

**1** Rinse, drain, and dry the whole herbs. Chop them finely (see p123) and place them in small dishes, ramekins, or mugs.

**2** Cover with dampened paper towels and chill for up to 3 days. To store for an extra couple of days, cover with a layer of plastic wrap.

# WHOLE HERBS IN THE FRIDGE

Many herbs, such as basil, flat-leaf parsley, chives, or tarragon can be chilled whole, but first rinse the herbs and pat them dry with a paper towel or a clean dish towel.

Dampen a sheet of absorbent paper towel. Gently squeeze out any excess water, and flatten. Moist paper towels will prevent the herbs from drying out.

**2** Fold and then wrap the paper towel fairly loosely around the stems. Alternatively, you could wrap the moistened paper towel around the whole sprig.

Slip the wrapped herbs into a freezer bag and flatten gently to remove some of the air. Seal the bag and chill in the refrigerator for up to a week.

*Jars of herbs You can also scrunch up the dampened paper towel and put it in a jar with the herbs. Seal with the lid and refrigerate.*

# FREEZING

Most herbs keep their flavor extremely well during freezing but their appearance tends to suffer. Frozen herbs work well in salad dressings, sauces, stuffings, toppings, soups, and in slowly cooked dishes, such as roasts and pot roasts. You can freeze herbs in oil or water.

*Flower cubes* *Pick edible flowers, such as borage, and freeze them individually in ice cube trays ready to use in drinks and to flavor syrups, custards, and gelatins.*

## HERB OIL MIXES

Various herbs and garlic freeze well with a little olive oil. Freeze the herbs singly or combined with others, such as basil with garlic; garlic with grated root ginger and Thai basil; parsley with garlic, thyme, and oregano; or sage with fennel.

**1** Coarsely chop the herbs in a food processor. Blend briefly. With the motor running, add enough olive oil to lightly coat the herbs (about 1 tbsp oil to 3 tbsp herbs).

**2** Spoon the mixture into very small freezer bags, seal them securely, label, and place in the freezer. Herbs in oil can be frozen for up to 4 months.

# HERB ICE CUBES

Ice cube trays are an easy way to store chopped herbs, such as chives, parsley, tarragon, dill, chervil, cilantro, or even green onions, in the freezer. Use them straight from frozen in hot liquids.

You can freeze finely chopped single herbs or herb combinations. Fill an ice cube tray to the brim with the herbs and pour water over just to cover. Freeze until solid, about 2 hours. Pop the frozen cubes out and slip a few at a time into freezer bags. Close, label, and place in the freezer until needed. Use within 6 months.

## FROZEN GARLIC ROLL

Chopped herbs, singly or mixed, as well as garlic, can be shaped into a roll and frozen without having to add water or oil. They can then be added to your cooking straight from the freezer.

**1** Peel and halve the cloves of 2 or 3 bulbs of very fresh garlic. Remove any green shoots in the cloves with the point of a knife and discard.

**2** Using the side of a large chef's knife, smash the garlic cloves flat by pressing down quickly and firmly on the flat side of the blade with the palm of your hand.

**3** Put the smashed cloves in the center of a piece of plastic wrap, keeping them well away from the edges.

**4** Bring up the long edges, and roll the cloves in the plastic wrap to make a cigar shape. Twist the ends to seal. Place in the freezer.

To use, open up at one end and expose some of the
arlic. Slice or shave off the amount you need. Reseal
nd return the roll to the freezer. Use within 4 months.

# DRYING

Drying is an ideal way to preserve the flavor of herbs with woody stalks and tougher leaves, such as bay leaf, thyme, and rosemary. Once dried, other herbs, such as mint and sage, taste noticeably different. Most home-dried herbs will, however, lose their flavor after six months as their essential oils evaporate.

## DRYING FLAT

Individual leaves, fronds, and small spriglets of herbs, such as thyme, rosemary, marjoram, oregano, fennel, dill, bay leaf, or sage, can be dried flat on a piece of cheesecloth stretched over a frame. Place them out of direct sunlight in a dry, airy room, such as an attic, for at least 2 weeks until their color fades a little and the herbs become slightly brittle.

**1** Pluck the herbs from their stem into separate leaves or small clusters. Place them flat on the cheesecloth in a single layer so they do not touch one another.

**2** Once dry (leave for at least 2 weeks), pack the herbs loosely in clean glass jars with tightly fitting lids. Seal the jar and store out of direct light. Use within 4–6 months.

## HANGING HERBS

Air circulates around herbs easily when they are hung to dry. Hang a few strips of unwaxed orange or lemon peel to dry on the line, too—their flavors mix well with dried herbs during cooking. Leave for at least 2 weeks until the color fades a little and the herbs are brittle.

**I** Make herb posies with 3–4 stems each of single herbs, such as bay leaf, fennel fronds, rosemary, or thyme. Avoid using more than one herb in a bundle, as different herbs have different drying times. Tie the bundles together with kitchen string.

**2** Fix the bundles to a line in an airy, dry room out of direct sunlight. After at least 2 weeks untie the herbs and store them in sealed jars. Use within 4–6 months.

## SEEDS

Fennel, dill, and coriander seeds, among others, can be home-dried for culinary use (and sowing). Dried seeds are best when used within 6 months before all their essential oils have evaporated.

**1** Plants make seeds after they flower. Select a strong-looking plant that has gone to seed and harvest it by cutting the stems just above the soil line (see p107).

**2** Bunch the stems together and tie them securely with string, leaving some extra for hanging them up. Hold the stems upside down to make sure they are secure.

**3** Cover the seedheads with cheesecloth (or a brown paper bag) and tie securely in place. Hang upside down in a dry, airy room out of direct sunlight.

**4** After a week or so the seeds will drop off the plant and into the cheesecloth. Carefully lift down the stems, shake them, and collect the seeds. Store in a paper bag.

## FLOWERS

Lavender, fennel, chamomile, marigold, or borage flowers are easy to dry for future use.

1 Remove whole stems of flowers from the plant. Cut off the flowers with scissors making sure that no stem is left attached.

2 Scatter on cheesecloth stretched over a frame. Leave in a dry place out of sunlight for 3 weeks until brittle. Store in a sealed jar and use within 6 months.

## CHILES

Dried chiles really hold their heat and flavor. Choose ripe blemish-free chiles for drying.

1 Thread a long piece of string through a very large needle. Pierce each chile through the stalk and thread each chile onto the string, leaving an extra length of string for hanging. Knot the bottom chile in place.

2 Hang the string of chiles in an airy room away from direct sunlight to dry. Use within 8 months for the best flavor.

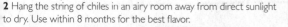

# HOW TO BRAID GARLIC

Garlic stalks must be dried before they can be braided. Harvest the bulbs in early summer before the outer leaves start to decay. Keep their long stalks intact but do not let them dry so much that they become brittle. There should still be a little moisture at the center of the stem.

**1** Spread the bulbs out on a flat surface in a dry, airy, sheltered place out of direct sunlight for 2–4 weeks.

**2** Give the bulbs a light brush to remove excess soil and then trim off the dried roots.

**3** Nestle 3 bulbs together. Secure them with kitchen string if you like to hold them in place.

**4** Repeat the 3-bulb pattern by setting a bulb straight on top and criss-crossing 2 more over that.

**5** Divide the stems into 3 strands of 2 stalks each to braid. Bring the 2 right-hand stems up over to the left.

**6** Repeat, crossing to the right using the central stem. Repeat a few more times and tie off in a knot at the end.

**7** Hang the braid in a well-ventilated but cold room, ideally 33–41°F (1–5°C) to prevent green shoots sprouting in the bulbs. The location is important because humidity and lack of ventilation will make the garlic moldy.

# COOK

You've transformed your garden, now
do the same to your food. Perk up salads,
spice up salsas, and pack a punch with
marinades and sauces; knowing how to
use homegrown herbs will guarantee
flavorsome food.

# PREPARATION

After harvesting your herbs wash, rinse, and dry them thoroughly. With most herbs the leaves must be separated from the stalks. Different herbs need different handling but tough stalks always need to be discarded.

## STRIPPING
For preparing herbs with tough stalks.

Hold one end of the stalk with both hands. Move the thumb and first finger of one hand down the stalk pinching firmly to strip off the leaves.

## PLUCKING
For preparing herbs with tender stalks.

Hold the bottom of the stalk in one hand and pull the fronds up and outward. Pluck the fronds from any remaining smaller stalks afterward.

## PICKING
For preparing watercress leaves.

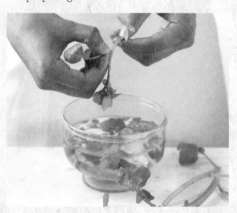

Separate watercress leaves and florets from the thick stalks. Discard the stalks and drop the leaves into ice-cold water to keep them fresh. Drain before using.

## SLICING
For roughly chopping leaves and fronds.

Using a large chef's knife, slice up and down with one hand while guiding the herbs with the other, fingertips folded back so only knuckles are near the knife.

# CHOPPING

Finely chopped herbs blend quickly into dressings, soups, and sauces. Coarsely chopped herbs keep their distinctive flavor and work well in slow cooking. Always rinse and dry the herbs before chopping. Use a very sharp chef's knife or, for large amounts, use a mezzaluna or food processor.

Grasp the handle of a large chef's knife. Hold the point of the blade with the fingers of your other hand. Chop by rocking the knife up and down in the herbs.

Hold a handle of the mezzaluna in each hand. Chop in a side-to-side rocking motion. Heap the herbs back into a pile from time to time with the blade.

# PILING

To save time, herbs with wide flat leaves, such as basil, sorrel, or mint can be piled up and sliced.

Gently stack the leaves underside-up. The more leaves you include in a stack, the less slicing you will need to do. Try not to bruise the herbs as you handle them.

2 Hold the stack firmly and slice with a large chef's knife into very thin shreds, keeping your fingertips well away from the blade.

## SNIPPING SMALL LEAVES

Small-leaved herbs, such as curly or flat-leaf parsley, chervil, fennel fronds, cilantro, or tarragon, can be conveniently snipped in a wide bowl using a pair of sharp kitchen scissors.

Wash and thoroughly dry the herbs. Strip, pluck, or pick the leaves and discard the stems. Place the leaves in a wide bowl. Support the bowl with one hand and snip the herbs with the scissors, working your way round the bowl.

## ROLLING AND SNIPPING LARGE LEAVES

Herbs with larger leaves, such as basil, sorrel, or mint, are easy to prepare by rolling them up and then snipping them with kitchen scissors. Be careful not to bruise the herbs as you handle them.

1 Gently stack a few large flat leaves, such as basil, sorrel, or mint, on top of one another underside-up. Roll them up securely into a cigar shape.

2 Hold the rolled herbs in one hand but keep your fingers back from the scissor blades. Snip through the pile into thin shreds.

## SMASHING

For extracting the flavor of garlic cloves.

Put a few cloves on a cutting board. Lay the blade flat on top of a clove, and press down quickly and firmly with the palm of your hand.

## BRUISING

For releasing essential oils in lemongrass.

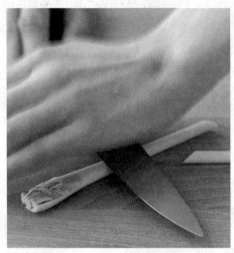

Put the trimmed lemongrass on a cutting board. Lay the blade flat on top and press down firmly with your palm. This method also works with bay leaves and citrus peel.

## POUNDING

A pestle and mortar is the best way to pound and mash herbs and seeds to release their flavors.

1 Put coarsely chopped or snipped herbs and seeds into the mortar. Pound straight down with the pestle until the herbs and seeds are smashed.

2 Beat the smashed mixture in a circular motion, mashing until you have a coarse purée. A pinch of sea salt and a tablespoon of olive oil helps the process.

## PREPARING CHILES

Seed your chiles before chopping them if you do not like them fiercely hot. Chopped chiles can then be placed in small freezer bags and frozen for up to 6 months.

**1** Lay the chile on a cutting board. Using a sharp chef's knife, chop off the stalk and discard. Slice down the middle. Scrape out the seeds and discard.

**2** Slice the chile flesh lengthwise into thin strips, skin-side down. Be sure to keep your fingertips away from the cutting edge of the knife.

**3** Turn the strips over and slice across the width until they are very finely chopped. Take care never to touch your face or eyes when working with chiles and wash your hands thoroughly afterward, or wear disposable plastic or latex gloves.

***Chiles*** *The heat level of chiles can range from mild to blisteringly hot.*

## GRATING

To get the most flavor from roots, such as horseradish or ginger, simply peel and grate them.

Slice off a chunk of fresh horseradish and peel the skin. Finely grate the amount of horseradish you need. Peeled roots can be frozen in a freezer bag and grated directly from the freezer. Reseal and return to the freezer immediately after use. Frozen horseradish and ginger will keep in the freezer for up to 6 months.

# FLAVORINGS

For tough, fibrous herbs, such as rosemary, thyme, and bay leaf, it's a good idea to remove the herbs before serving after their flavors have infused into your cooking. You can brush ingredients with herbs, mix herbs in a bouquet garni, or put herbs, seeds, and peels in a cheesecloth pouch.

## BOUQUETS GARNIS

A staple in French cooking, these aromatic bunches of herbs enhance the flavor of slow-cooked dishes. Add them to a stew or pot roast before cooking, and discard before serving.

**Herb brush** *Dip herb sprigs in olive oil and brush roasts during cooking. Discard after use.*

*For stronger flavors, make a large bouquet garni, using a generous handful of each of the herbs*

*Fresh bay leaf holds the bundle together and adds flavor*

*Leave enough string to tie a loop to hang over the pan so you can remove it easily after cooking*

*Wrap the string several times around the bunch and make a secure knot*

## ЗHEESECLOTH POUCHES

ust like a bouquet garni in a bag, you can fill a cheesecloth pouch with fresh or dried herbs.

Cut a piece of clean cheesecloth into a square ٦easuring 4 × 4 in (10 × 10 cm).

**2** Place your selection of aromatic flavorings in the middle of the cheesecloth square. Use more herbs for a stronger flavor.

Bring up the corners of the cheesecloth to enclose ٦e flavorings and tie securely with a piece of kitchen ٠ring. Leave enough string to retrieve the pouch.

### BEST COMBINATIONS

Lots of herbs complement each other when used together for flavoring particular ingredients. Here are some reliable combinations:

**Classic Meat** Parsley, thyme, and bay leaf

**Fish** Parsley, thyme, lemon peel, and dill or fennel

**Poultry** Parsley, tarragon, thyme, and orange peel

**Vegetables** Sage, parsley, and marjoram or oregano

# THE RECIPES

All your efforts in the garden, on the balcony, or on the window ledge have paid off and now it is time to get cooking. Fresh herbs shine in so many main and side dishes, such as soups, sauces, and salsas, and they enliven other ingredients in marinades, rubs, and coatings. The marinade, rub, and coating recipes do not feature cooking times— the way you cook your poultry, meat, or fish is entirely up to you.

## BUTTERS

Simple combinations of chopped herbs and soft butter are an easy and versatile way to add a fresh aromatic touch to cooked meats. To store butters, shape into a sausage, wrap in plastic wrap, and twist the ends to seal. Keep in the fridge for up to 1 week or in the freezer for up to 3 months. To use, cut off disks as needed straight from the fridge or freezer.

### WATERCRESS BUTTER

**Peppery watercress and butter are a mouthwatering mix for grilled meats and fish. This butter can also be used as a sandwich spread.**

**MAKES** 7 OZ (200 G)   **PREP** 20 MINS

3½ oz (100 g) watercress, rinsed and dried
sea salt and freshly ground black pepper

3½ oz (100 g) unsalted butter, softened
   and cut into 10–12 pieces
2 tsp lemon juice

1 Put the watercress into a colander, pick the leaves, and discard the stalks (see p122).
2 Place the leaves in the small bowl of a food processor in batches. Season with a little salt and more generously with pepper. Pulse quickly until finely chopped.
3 Add the butter to the watercress, and drizzle in the lemon juice. Whiz until smooth, or beat with a wooden spoon, and transfer to a small dish. Cover and chill until ready to use.

## OREGANO BUTTER

Use to add an evocative Mediterranean touch to roasted vegetables and bruschetta

MAKES 3½OZ (100 G)  PREP 20 MIN

I scant tbsp groundnut or mild olive oil
3½oz (100 g) unsalted butter, softened
  and cut

3 tbsp oregano, finely chopped
I garlic clove
sea salt and freshly ground black pepper

1 Place a layer of paper towels on a plate. Put the oil and 2 tsp of the butter in a small non-stick frying pan over medium heat. Add the oregano and garlic and stir-fry for 2 minutes. Remove the oregano and garlic, and spread them over the plate.
2 Blend together the rest of the butter and the drained oregano and garlic in a food processor, pestle and mortar, or in a bowl with a fork. Season lightly with salt and pepper.
3 Transfer to a small dish, cover, and chill until ready to use.

## TARRAGON BUTTER

This butter, with its lemony herbal flavor, is excellent when served melted over white fish, such as mahi mahi, cod, catfish, halibut, and tilapia.

MAKES 3½OZ (100 G)  PREP 15 MINS

3 tbsp tarragon, finely chopped
sea salt and freshly ground black pepper

3½oz (100 g) very soft unsalted butter
2 tsp lemon juice

1 Put the tarragon into a small bowl. Season lightly with salt and pepper, and add the butter and lemon juice.
2 Mash everything together until creamy. Transfer to a small dish and chill until ready to use.

Cook's note To make the butter very soft, dice it and then mash it in a bowl with a fork over medium-hot water, or soften in the microwave on low for 1 minute.

# SNAIL BUTTER

Though this is the traditional butter to serve sizzling hot with snails, it is also delicious with chicken or fish.

**MAKES** 5½ OZ (150 G)  **PREP** 15 MINS

4½ oz (125 g) very soft unsalted butter
2½ tbsp lemon juice
3 tbsp finely chopped flat-leaf or curly parsley

4 garlic cloves
sea salt and freshly ground black pepper

**1** Mash together the butter and lemon juice until well mixed and creamy.
**2** Beat in the parsley. Smash the garlic cloves with the flat of a knife, peel, sprinkle with salt, and crush in a pestle and mortar. Beat into the butter. Transfer to a small dish, cover, and chill for up to 3 days until ready to use. Do not freeze.

# MONTPELLIER BUTTER

A pungent butter with a mild Tabasco kick. Serve it with grilled meat or fish.

**MAKES** 7 OZ (200 G)  **PREP** 30 MINS

2 shallots, chopped
1 tbsp each chopped flat-leaf (or curly) parsley, sorrel, cilantro (or chervil), tarragon, chives, and spinach (or watercress)
2 cured anchovy fillets, drained of oil and chopped
2 small dill pickles, chopped
1 tbsp capers, drained

1 garlic clove, smashed, peeled, and crushed
4½ oz (125 g) very soft unsalted butter
3 tbsp olive oil
sea salt and freshly ground black pepper
2 tsp white wine vinegar or tarragon vinegar (see p135)
a few drops Tabasco (optional)

**1** Bring a small pan of water to a boil. Add the shallots and the chopped herbs. Blanch for a minute, pour into a sieve, drain, refresh with cold water, drain well, and pat with the palm of your hand to extract excess moisture.
**2** Spread the herbs and shallots over a plate lined with a double layer of paper towels. Press dry with more paper towels.
**3** Using a food processor equipped with a small bowl, blend the herb and shallot mixture together with the anchovies, pickles, capers, garlic, and butter. Season with salt and pepper, scrape the sides of the bowl with a spatula, and trickle in the olive oil with the motor running.
**4** Taste and adjust the seasoning. Stir in the vinegar and Tabasco, if using.
**5** Transfer to a small dish, cover, and chill for at least 1 hour or up to a week. Do not freeze.

# OILS AND VINEGARS

Herb oils and vinegars are the best substitute for fresh herbs. Use impeccably clean sterilized bottles and a good quality oil or vinegar. Some oils are made by adding an ingredient, such as a chile, to fruity olive oil.

## ROSEMARY OIL

This oil is a kitchen treasure for drizzling over chicken and fish.

**MAKES** 8FL OZ (250 ML) **PREP** 20 MINS **COOK** 15 MINS

2 garlic cloves, unpeeled
6 sprigs of rosemary, leaves only

8fl oz (250 ml) fruity olive oil
3 small attractive sprigs of rosemary

**1** Blanch the garlic for 3 minutes in a small pan of boiling water. Remove from the pan and refresh in cold water. Drain it, pat it dry, and peel.

**2** Smash the rosemary leaves and garlic with the flat of a large kitchen knife (see p125). Put them into a small heavy pan, and pour in the oil. Bring to a simmer over a low heat, pushing down the leaves and garlic with a wooden spoon to extract their flavor. Cook and stir for 2–3 minutes. Take off the heat and leave until cold, still stirring and mashing occasionally.

**3** Meanwhile, blanch the 3 rosemary sprigs for 2 minutes in boiling water. Refresh them in cold water, then drain and dry them.

**4** Put the sprigs into a sterilized bottle (see p176). Line a funnel with dampened clean cheesecloth, and place it in the neck of the bottle. Pour the oil slowly into the bottle. Seal and keep in a cool place. Use within 6 weeks.

## TARRAGON VINEGAR

Use this vinegar in dressings or boil it up with diced shallot for a sauce.

**MAKES** 16FL OZ (500 ML) **PREP** 20 MINS **INFUSE** 24 HOURS

16fl oz (500 ml) white wine or cider vinegar
5 sprigs tarragon, plus 2–3 sprigs to finish

garlic clove
6 peppercorns

**1** In a sterilized jar (see p176) combine the vinegar with the 5 sprigs of tarragon, garlic, and peppercorns. Cover, shake well, and leave to infuse for at least 24 hours or until the tarragon discolors, shaking from time to time.

**2** Put 2 or 3 fresh tarragon sprigs in a new sterilized bottle. Strain the infused vinegar through a cheesecloth-lined sieve into a jug. Discard the flavorings. Pour the vinegar into the bottle and seal. Keep in a cool place. Use after 48 hours and within 2 months.

# RUBS

A rub is a mixture of herbs patted onto a main ingredient just before cooking, enhancing the aromatic appeal of a range of dishes. Remember that cooking changes the flavor of herbs. When roasting, cover loosely with foil so the herbs do not dry out too much. For added flavor, add extra fresh herbs right at the end of cooking.

## PARSLEY, TARRAGON, AND LEMON THYME RUB

This mix of herbs is perfect with roast chicken—try placing a little under the skin.

**FOR** I MEDIUM CHICKEN OR 2 POUSSINS **SERVES** 4 **PREP** 15 MINS

I tbsp finely chopped flat-leaf or curly parsley
2 tsp dried tarragon
2 stalks lemon thyme, leaves stripped, stems discarded

I tsp finely grated lemon zest
I tsp sea salt
¼ tsp freshly ground black pepper

Mix all the ingredients together in a cup. Scatter the mixture all over the chicken, patting it in gently. If roasting, sprinkle over fruity olive oil or dot with soft butter.

**Variations** To stuff the chicken, use the same herb mixture and no salt. Halve the quantities, add 1 heaped tbsp fresh bread crumbs, and stir into 7 oz (200 g) sausage meat or 7 oz (200 g) finely chopped fresh figs or apricots. Stir in 1 egg and pack loosely inside the chicken.

## FENNEL AND THYME RUB

The lemon juice moistens the herbs in this rub. Use with sea bass or red mullet.

**FOR** I LB 5OZ (600 G) FILLET OR 2 LB (900 G) WHOLE FISH **SERVES** 4 **PREP** 15 MINS

½ tbsp finely chopped flat-leaf or curly parsley
2 tsp dried fennel or dill seeds, crushed
2 stalks thyme, leaves stripped, stems discarded

I tbsp lemon juice
¼ tsp freshly ground white pepper

Mix the herbs and seeds in a cup. Stir in the lemon juice and white pepper. Scatter all over the fish (the lemon juice helps them stick to the fish), and smooth in gently.

**Cook's note** For a whole fish, use the same herb mix to flavor the cavity. Put in a shallow bowl. Slice half a lemon, dip the slices in the mixture, and slip inside the cavity of the fish.

# SAGE, JUNIPER, AND BAY LEAF RUB

Aromatic juniper, sage, and bay leaf work well with strongly flavored game and pork.

**FOR** 1¾ LB (800 G) MEAT **SERVES** 4 **PREP** 15 MINS

1 tbsp dried sage, crushed
1 tsp juniper berries
2 bay leaves, finely snipped
2 stalks thyme
1 tsp salt

1 garlic clove, crushed
1 tsp finely grated orange zest
1 tsp coarsely ground black pepper
5½ oz (150 g) mascarpone cheese
(use this for pork roast only)

Mix all the ingredients together in a cup. (For pork roast, add the mascarpone cheese.) Scatter the mixture all over the meat and pat it in lightly. If roasting, sprinkle over fruity olive oil or dot with butter. Scatter over a few fresh bay leaves toward the end of cooking.

# OREGANO, CITRUS, AND ROSEMARY RUB

Woody, citrussy flavors set off the sweet richness of lamb in this fragrant rub.

**FOR** 1¾ LB (800 G) LAMB **SERVES** 4 **PREP** 15 MINS

1 tsp chopped oregano or ½ tsp dried oregano
2 tsp finely grated lemon zest
small garlic clove, crushed
½ tsp ground cumin

1 tsp chopped rosemary leaves
1 tbsp chopped cilantro
sea salt and freshly ground black pepper

Mix all the ingredients together in a cup. Scatter all over the meat, patting it in gently. Just before cooking, season with salt and pepper. If roasting, sprinkle over fruity olive oil. Toward the end of cooking, sprinkle over 2 tbsp lemon juice and scatter over some chopped oregano.

# PERSILLADE

Add persillade to slow-cooked dishes at the end of cooking to liven them up.

**SERVES** 4 **PREP** 10 MINS

3 tbsp finely chopped flat-leaf or curly parsley
1 or 2 garlic cloves, crushed
sea salt and freshly ground black pepper

Mix the parsley with the garlic. Season with salt and pepper and stir lightly into pot roasts, stews, and casseroles after you have taken the dish off the heat.

**Variations** For Italian gremolata, add 2 tsp finely grated citrus zest to the mixture. For a gratin dish, stir 3 tbsp fresh bread crumbs into persillade or gremolata, sprinkle over the gratin, drizzle with olive oil or dot with butter. Continue baking for 10–15 minutes.

# COATINGS

Halfway between simple dry rubs and wet marinades, coatings wrap meat and fish in an aromatic layer. Their flavors blend in with the ingredients as they cook and add a nice touch of texture to the dish.

## SAGE AND PARSLEY COATING (PICTURED)
The highly fragrant herbs in this coating work wonders on poultry.

COATS I MEDIUM CHICKEN OR 2 POUSSINS **SERVES** 4 **PREP** 20 MINS **CHILL** 30 MINS

2 garlic cloves, smashed
sea salt
8 sage leaves, chopped
2 tbsp chopped flat-leaf parsley
I tsp thyme

I tsp summer or winter savory, chopped
I tsp Szechuan peppercorns
I ½ oz (40–50 g) butter, very soft
2 tbsp mild olive oil

**1** Place the garlic, a little sea salt, sage, and parsley into a mortar and mash.
**2** Add the thyme, savory, and peppercorns and continue mashing together.
**3** Add the butter and the oil. Pound down with the pestle a few times, and then mix the ingredients together using a circular movement (see p125).
**4** Put the poultry in a dish. Spoon half of the mixture onto it. Smooth the paste over the whole surface and press down gently. Turn the poultry over, and repeat until coated.
**5** Cover loosely with plastic wrap and chill for at least 30 minutes.

## CILANTRO AND MINT COATING
This robust paste gives shoulder of lamb a warm Mediterranean spiciness.

COATS I LB 5OZ (600 G) LAMB **SERVES** 4 **PREP** 15 MINS **CHILL** 30 MINS

2 garlic cloves, smashed and peeled
I tsp cumin seeds
½ tsp ground cumin
½ tsp ground coriander
I tbsp chopped fresh cilantro

I tsp dried mint
I tsp finely grated lemon zest
3 tbsp fruity olive oil
2 tsp rosemary
sea salt and freshly ground black pepper

**1** Blend the garlic, cumin, coriander, cilantro, mint, and lemon zest in a food processor using the pulse mode. Blend in the olive oil. Stop the motor.
**2** Stir the rosemary into the mixture, and season with pepper.
**3** Put the lamb on a dish. Spoon half the mixture onto it. Smooth it over the whole surface and press down gently. Turn the lamb over, and repeat until coated.
**4** Cover the lamb loosely with plastic wrap and chill for at least 30 minutes. Season with salt before cooking.

# HORSERADISH AND BAY LEAF COATING

All the classic combinations for beef—horseradish, bay leaves, mustard seeds, and peppercorns—are here, giving the coating lots of texture and a fiery kick.

COATS 1 LB 5OZ (600 G) BEEF **SERVES** 4 **PREP** 15 MINS **CHILL** 30 MINS

1 garlic clove
1 tsp black peppercorns
1 tsp mustard seeds
2 tsp freshly grated horseradish
2 finely chopped bay leaves

1 tbsp finely chopped flat-leaf
or curly parsley
1 tbsp mild olive oil
2 tbsp very soft butter
sea salt

1 Use a pestle and mortar (or, if you prefer, blend the ingredients quickly in a food processor using the pulse mode). Put the garlic and peppercorns in the bowl. Smash down with the pestle to crush. Add the mustard seeds and grated horseradish, bay leaves, and parsley. Pound down with the pestle until smashed and mixed.
2 Add the oil and butter, pound down a few times, then beat to mix using a circular movement (see p125).
3 Put the beef in the center of a plate. Spoon half the mixture onto the center of the beef. Spread the mixture outward, smoothing it over the whole surface with your hands. Turn over, spoon the rest of the mixture over the beef, and smooth it down until the beef is completely coated.
4 Cover loosely with plastic wrap and chill for at least 30 minutes to give the flavors time to release into the beef, or longer if you prefer more developed flavors (overnight is ideal). Season with salt just before cooking.

*Horseradish*
*Used in moderation, horseradish*
*adds a pungent note to celery root,*
*salmon, or beef dishes.*

# DILL AND CILANTRO COATING

This coating is for salmon, and gives it an attractive warm red-brown color.

**COATS** 1½LB (700 G) SALMON FILLET **SERVES** 4 **PREP** 15 MINS **CHILL** 15 MINS

2 tbsp chopped dill fronds
1 tbsp chopped cilantro
1 tbsp chopped basil
½ tsp coarsely ground white pepper
1 tbsp soy sauce
1 tsp superfine sugar or honey
¼ tsp hot paprika

1 tbsp mild olive oil, plus a little extra to finish
1 tbsp very soft butter, plus a little extra to finish
2 tsp finely chopped chives
1 tbsp lemon juice and 1 tsp finely grated zest
sea salt

**1** Put the dill, cilantro, basil, white pepper, soy sauce, sugar or honey, and paprika in the small bowl of a food processor. Blend using the pulse mode. Whiz in the olive oil and butter and stop the motor.

**2** Stir the chives and the lemon juice and zest into the mixture, and adjust the seasoning to taste.

**3** Spoon half the mixture over the center of the salmon fillet. Spread over the whole surface using the palms of your hands. Turn over, spoon the rest of the mixture over the salmon, and smooth down until completely coated.

**4** Cover the salmon loosely with plastic wrap. Chill for at least 15 minutes to give the flavors time to develop. Dot with a little extra butter or add a sprinkling of olive oil just before cooking.

**Cilantro**
*Versatile cilantro is the traditional flavoring for fish dishes in many parts of the world.*

# MARINADES

The liquid in marinades, usually alcohol or citrus juice, tenderizes and part-cooks the meat. At the same time, the herbs impart their flavor. Be generous and add plenty of herbs to the infusion.

## BAY LEAF, LOVAGE, AND JUNIPER MARINADE

This marinade brings out the very best in venison and beef. For tougher cuts and more mature meat, leave it to marinate for up to 48 hours.

COATS 2¼–3⅓ LB (1–1.5 KG) MEAT  SERVES 4–6  PREP 15 MINS  COOK 20 MINS  MARINATE 4 HOURS

1 garlic clove
4 bay leaves
4–6 sprigs flat-leaf parsley, both leaves and
   stalks, chopped
2 sprigs lovage, chopped
1 green onion (or 2 spring onions), chopped

1 shallot, roughly chopped
6 juniper berries
12 black peppercorns
2 in (5 cm) piece dried orange peel
1¼ pints (600 ml) smooth, mellow,
   good-quality red wine

1 Smash the garlic with the flat of a knife, then peel and crush in a pestle and mortar. Smash the bay leaves with a kitchen mallet. Put these in a medium pan and add the herbs and chopped onion and shallot. Add the juniper berries, peppercorns, and orange peel. Pour in the red wine and 8fl oz (250 ml) water. Bring to a boil over high heat.

2 Once it is boiling, reduce the heat and partially cover. Let it simmer for 5 minutes to allow the raw alcohol taste of the wine to disappear.

3 Take off the heat and leave to cool. Put the beef or venison in a slightly larger bowl or non-metallic container big enough to hold the meat and the marinade. Pour the marinade over the meat and turn it over a couple of times. Cover and refrigerate for at least 4 hours (ideally overnight) to give time for the flavors to infuse and the wine to tenderize the meat. Turn the meat 2–3 times during marinating.

4 When you are ready to cook the meat, remove the dish from the fridge. Lift out the meat and drain it well. If you intend to fry or roast the meat, pat it dry with paper towels. Push the marinade through a sieve into a jug. It will be highly aromatic and makes an ideal cooking liquid or base for stock or gravy.

# CITRUS AND BASIL MARINADE

This marinade is for pork. Because it roasts in the oven with the meat the marinade reduces to a thick syrupy sauce.

**COATS** 1LB 5OZ (600 G) PORK TENDERLOIN **SERVES** 4 **PREP** 15 MINS **MARINATE** 1 HOUR

juice of 2 unwaxed oranges
finely grated zest of 1 unwaxed orange
3 tbsp soy sauce
12 sweet basil leaves, finely chopped
12–15 chives, finely chopped
1 in (3 cm) piece fresh root ginger, grated

2 garlic cloves
1 tsp coriander seeds
14fl oz (400 ml) plain yogurt
2 tbsp mild olive oil
sea salt and freshly ground black pepper

**1** Put the orange juice and zest in a bowl large enough to hold the pork and the marinade. Stir in the soy sauce and add the basil, chives, and grated ginger.
**2** Pound the garlic cloves and coriander seeds using a pestle and mortar or the flat side of a large knife (see p125) and add them to the bowl. Stir to mix. Then stir in the yogurt and oil. Season with salt and pepper to taste.
**3** Add the meat to the marinade. Using your hands or a spoon, turn the pork over several times until it is evenly coated. Cover the dish with plastic wrap and leave in the fridge to marinate for at least 1 hour before cooking. Leave it to marinate longer if you prefer stronger flavors.

**Variation** This also tastes wonderful with chicken, and coats 4–6 leg or breast portions or 1 whole medium chicken.

*Sweet basil*
*Eggs, poultry, pork,*
*peppers, and tomatoes*
*are all enhanced by basil.*

# NO-COOK MARINADES

Marinades can be used to cold-cook very fresh fish and vegetables. The process also develops and changes the flavors of the herbs. Add more fresh herbs just before serving to deepen the flavor.

## DILLED SMOKED HADDOCK

**Use fresh undyed smoked haddock fillet for this tangy appetizer.**

SERVES 6 AS A STARTER  PREP 15 MINS  MARINATE 1–2 HOURS  FINISH 10 MINS

1 tsp chopped dill fronds, plus 1½ tsp to finish
2 tsp finely chopped flat-leaf or curly parsley
1 tsp finely chopped chives, plus 1 tsp to finish
1 tsp finely chopped stripped thyme leaves
juice and finely grated zest of 1 small lemon
1 tbsp fruity olive oil, plus 3 tbsp to finish
14 oz (400 g) smoked haddock fillet

**To serve**
1 lemon, cut into wedges
6 slices toasted bread
1 garlic clove, peeled and halved
butter for spreading

1 Put the herbs in a shallow bowl. Add the lemon juice and zest, and 1 tbsp of the olive oil. Stir well and set aside while you prepare the fish.

2 Wipe the fish clean. Remove any remaining bones. Shred with a fork. Add to the herb marinade and stir to coat. Cover and chill for 1–2 hours.

3 Transfer the fish to a large sieve, and drain well. Pat gently dry with paper towels (don't worry if some of the herbs come off). Transfer to a serving bowl, sprinkle over the 3 tbsp olive oil and the reserved herbs. Toss gently. Serve at once with lemon wedges and toast rubbed with the cut sides of a garlic clove and lightly buttered.

## CUCUMBER WITH TARRAGON AND CREAM

**Tarragon's licorice flavor is perfect with marinated cucumber and cream.**

SERVES 4 AS A STARTER  PREP 15 MINS  STAND 30 MINS  FINISH 10 MINS

1 large firm unblemished cucumber, peeled and thinly sliced
2 tbsp coarse sea salt
½ tsp superfine sugar

1 tbsp chopped tarragon, plus 2 tsp to finish
4 tbsp heavy cream, or 3 tbsp sour cream
freshly ground black pepper

1 Put the cucumber in a colander. Mix the salt, sugar, and tarragon, and sprinkle over the cucumber. Toss, then put a weighted plate on top. Leave for 30 minutes.

2 Rinse in plenty of cold water to get rid of any excess salt, drain well, and press down hard to extract all the moisture. Pat dry with paper towels.

3 Transfer to a serving bowl. Spoon over the cream, toss lightly, and scatter over the reserved tarragon. Stir lightly, season with pepper, and serve. This dish can be refrigerated overnight.

# ZUCCHINI WITH CHIVE MARINADE

Chive and thyme flavor the zucchini while the marinade draws out their excess moisture to create a flavorful and succulent dish.

**SERVES** 4 AS A STARTER **PREP** 20 MINS **STAND** 40 MINS **FINISH** 10 MINS

14 oz (400 g) small firm unblemished zucchini
4 tbsp fruity olive oil
2 tbsp lemon juice and 1 tbsp finely grated zest
1 tsp finely chopped chives, plus 2 tsp to finish

1 tsp finely chopped flat-leaf or curly parsley plus 1 tsp to finish
1 tsp finely chopped thyme
sea salt and freshly ground black pepper

1 Rinse the zucchini, pat them dry, and then top and tail them. Using a vegetable peeler, shave lengthwise into thin strips (it doesn't matter if some strips are just peel or a little thicker). Reserve on a plate lined with a double layer of paper towel.

2 In a bowl, mix 1 tbsp of the olive oil with the lemon juice and zest, chives, parsley, and thyme, and season lightly with salt and pepper. Add the zucchini strips and toss to coat. Leave to stand in a cool place for at least 40 minutes.

3 Put into a colander. Drain well, pressing down gently, then pat dry with paper towels.

4 Transfer to a serving bowl. Spoon over the reserved olive oil, chives, and parsley, and toss lightly. Taste and season with salt and pepper. Serve at room temperature.

# MUSHROOMS À LA GRECQUE

Chervil and cilantro add a fresh herb flavor to this easy appetizer.

**SERVES** 4–6 AS A STARTER **PREP** 20 MINS **MARINATE** 4 HOURS **FINISH** 10 MINS

4 tbsp fruity olive oil, plus 2 tbsp to finish
1 garlic clove, smashed, peeled, and crushed
3 tbsp lemon juice and 2 tsp finely grated zest
2 tbsp finely chopped flat-leaf parsley
1 tsp crushed coriander seeds
1 tbsp chopped chervil, plus 1 tbsp to finish

14 oz (400 g) very fresh white round cap mushrooms, wiped clean with damp a paper towel and thinly sliced
sea salt and freshly ground black pepper
1 tbsp chopped cilantro
2 tsp sherry vinegar

1 In a bowl, combine the olive oil, crushed garlic, lemon juice and zest, parsley, coriander seeds, and chervil.

2 Add the sliced mushrooms to the bowl and season lightly with salt and pepper. Toss, cover, and leave to marinate in the fridge for 4 hours.

3 Place the mixture into a colander, and drain off any excess liquid. Stir in the extra 2 tbsp of olive oil and the vinegar, and season. Scatter over the reserved chervil and the chopped cilantro. Serve soon at room temperature.

# SALSAS

Nothing awakens the taste buds like a salsa, whether it is hot and fiery or luxuriously creamy and cooling. Use salsas for dipping or pouring, with grilled seafood, poultry, or pork, or with raw vegetables.

## LEMONGRASS AND CHILE SALSA

This salsa transforms grilled fish or skewers of barbecued white meat.

**SERVES** 6 **PREP** 20 MINS **CHILL** 1 HOUR

2 stalks lemongrass, outer leaves discarded
2 heaped tbsp chopped Thai basil,
  plus 6 extra leaves to finish
1 tsp freshly grated root ginger
1 whole red chile, seeded and finely chopped

1 tbsp runny honey or 1 tbsp sugar
3 tbsp soy sauce
2 tsp fish sauce
6 tbsp lime juice

**1** Slice off the tops of the lemongrass stalks and discard them. Bash down on the bulb ends with the side of a large knife or pound using a kitchen mallet (see p125). Chop very finely and place in a bowl.

**2** Add the basil, the ginger, and the chile.

**3** Pour in the honey or sugar, the soy sauce, fish sauce, and the lime juice, and stir well. Cover and chill for at least 1 hour to give the flavors time to develop.

**4** Just before serving stir in the reserved whole basil leaves.

*Chile*
*A touch of chile adds a magic heat to*
*salsas and curries and brings out the*
*flavors of other herbs and spices.*

## AVOCADO, PAPRIKA, AND LIME SALSA

Nutty avocado with a hint of spice and citrus make a good side dish for hot Tex-Mex recipes and grilled fish or poultry.

**SERVES** 4–6 **PREP** 20 MINS **CHILL** 30 MINS

2 ripe vine tomatoes
2 ripe Hass avocados, halved, pitted, and peeled
juice of 1 lime
4–5 sprigs cilantro

3–4 sprigs flat-leaf parsley
sea salt and freshly ground black pepper
¼ tsp hot paprika
1 tbsp mild olive oil

1 Place the tomatoes into boiling water for 1 minute. Lift them out with a large spoon and when they are cool enough to handle, peel and halve them. Scoop out and discard the seeds, remove the tomato core, and cut into small dice. Set aside.

2 Cut the avocado flesh into small dice about the same size as the diced tomatoes. Put in a bowl, pour over the lime juice, and toss gently. Add the herbs, season with salt and pepper, and then add the paprika.

3 Stir the diced tomatoes into the mixture. Chill for 30 minutes or until ready to use. Stir through the olive oil, and season before serving.

## ARUGULA AND MASCARPONE SALSA

This is a tasty dip for garlicky toast, crudité batons, and steamed new potatoes.

**SERVES** 4–6 **PREP** 20 MINS **CHILL** 30 MINS

1¾ oz (50 g) arugula
2 tbsp roughly chopped chives
2 tbsp chervil
sea salt and freshly ground black pepper

3½ oz (100 g) mascarpone
3½ oz (100 g) ricotta
1 tbsp balsamic vinegar

1 Put the arugula, half the chives, and half the chervil in the small bowl of a food processor and season lightly with salt and pepper. Pulse briefly. Add the mascarpone and ricotta. Pulse again to mix but do not overprocess.

2 Transfer to a bowl, cover, and chill for 30 minutes or until ready to use. Stir in the balsamic vinegar, adjust the seasoning, and add the remaining chives and chervil.

# DILL, WATERCRESS, CAPER, AND TOMATO SALSA

Fresh and citrussy, this salsa is fabulous with grilled white fish or shrimp.

**SERVES** 4–6 **PREP** 15 MINS **CHILL** 30 MINS

2 tbsp chopped dill fronds
1¾ oz (50 g) picked watercress leaves, chopped
9 baby cherry tomatoes, halved
1 heaped tbsp capers, drained

juice and finely grated zest of ½ lemon
sea salt and freshly ground black pepper
3 tbsp fruity olive oil

1 Put the dill and watercress in a bowl. Gently squeeze the halved cherry tomatoes to discard some of the seeds, slice them again to quarter them, and add them to the bowl. Stir in the capers (if they are large, chop them first) and lemon juice and zest. Chill for 30 minutes or until ready to use.
2 Stir, season with salt and pepper, and drizzle with olive oil. Stir again before serving.

**Variation** For a chile, cilantro, and red onion salsa, use the same method but replace the dill with 2 tbsp chopped cilantro. Replace the tomatoes with 1 small finely chopped red onion and, instead of using the capers, add 1 heaped tbsp chopped fresh walnut halves or pecan kernels. Drizzle with 1½ tbsp olive oil and 1½ tbsp walnut oil.

**Dill**
*Dill fronds give a lovely
parsley-licorice flavor to a
wide range of dishes.*

# SALADS

Fresh herbs and flowers add excitement and texture to everyday salad ingredients. Be creative, and use whatever is in season, and remember—the fresher the better. Tear everything into bite-sized pieces.

## DANDELION, ARUGULA, AND FLOWER SALAD

Dress this exuberant pretty salad at the last minute and as lightly as possible.

SERVES 4  PREP 15 MINS

### For the dressing
4 tbsp groundnut, sunflower, or grapeseed oil, plus 1 tbsp to finish
sea salt and freshly ground black pepper
1 tbsp tarragon or white wine vinegar
½ tsp superfine sugar
4 lovage leaves, finely chopped

### For the salad
4½ oz (125 g) lightly packed young tender dandelion greens, rinsed and dried
3 oz (80–90 g) arugula, loosely torn
3 oz (80–90 g) pea shoots, loosely torn
2 tbsp chopped flat-leaf parsley
2 tbsp chopped chervil
1 tbsp small mint leaves
1 tbsp finely chopped chives
½ cup edible flowers, such as nasturtium or chive flowers, or English violet or pansy flower petals

1 Select a wide shallow salad bowl and prepare the dressing. Pour in the oil and season with salt and pepper. Whisk in the vinegar and sugar, and stir in the lovage.
2 Loosely tear up half the dandelion greens, and drop them into the bowl. Scatter half the arugula and half the pea shoots over the dandelion greens. Then add half the parsley, chervil, and mint. Do not toss.
3 Scatter over the remaining leaves, still without tossing.
4 Just before serving, scatter in the chives and flowers. Sprinkle over the reserved 1 tbsp of oil and season lightly.
5 Toss gently to coat the leaves, herbs, and flowers. Serve as soon as possible.

***Dandelion***
*With its slightly bitter flavor, raw dandelion is best added in moderation.*

# HERB TABBOULEH

Here is an intensively herby version of tabbouleh, a Middle Eastern classic.

**SERVES** 4 **PREP** 25 MINS

### For the dressing

I garlic clove, smashed, peeled, and crushed
sea salt and freshly ground black pepper
½ tsp five-spice powder
I tbsp lemon juice and I tsp finely grated
  unwaxed lemon zest
I tbsp pomegranate molasses or balsamic
  vinegar
4 tbsp fruity olive oil

### For the salad

2½ oz (75 g) fine bulgur wheat
6 tbsp chopped flat-leaf parsley
I tbsp finely chopped mint
I tbsp chopped cilantro
4 spring onions, finely chopped
4 baby cherry tomatoes, chopped

**1** Make the dressing in the bottom of a salad bowl. Mix the garlic with a little salt, the five-spice powder, lemon juice and zest, and the pomegranate molasses or balsamic vinegar. Whisk in the olive oil and season with salt and pepper to taste. Leave to stand while you prepare the ingredients for the salad.

**2** Put the bulgur in a shallow bowl, cover with hot water, and leave to swell for 2 minutes. Pour into a sieve, drain, and refresh with plenty of cold water, rubbing the bulgur grains between your fingers. Shake the bulgur and then drain well.

**3** Put the bulgur into the bowl with the dressing mixture. Add the parsley, mint, cilantro, spring onions, and tomatoes. Toss just before serving and season with salt and pepper.

**Variation** You can add 2 or 3 tbsp pomegranate seeds for a crunchy jewel-like finish.

***Flat-leaf parsley***
*A true kitchen essential, flat-leaf parsley can be trusted to improve the flavor of practically any savory dish.*

# SHEPHERD'S SALAD

Also called Arabic salad, this is a popular dish in Turkey and the Middle East.

SERVES 4  PREP 20 MINS

**For the dressing**
½ garlic clove, crushed
½ tsp sweet paprika
½ tsp ground sumac
½ tsp superfine sugar
½ tsp ground cumin
2 tbsp lemon juice and 1 tsp finely grated
  unwaxed lemon zest
7 tbsp fruity olive oil
sea salt and freshly ground black pepper

**For the salad**
1 large cucumber, peeled
15 baby cherry tomatoes
1 head sweet romaine or soft lettuce
12 black olives, pitted and chopped
3 spring onions, chopped
2 tbsp chopped flat-leaf parsley
2 tbsp chopped purslane or arugula
2 tbsp chopped cilantro
2 tbsp chopped mint

1 Make the dressing in the bottom of a salad bowl. Mix all the ingredients for the dressing and season with salt and pepper to taste. Leave the mixture to rest while you prepare the salad ingredients.

2 Cut the cucumber into 4 segments lengthwise, scoop out the seeds, and discard them. Cut the flesh into small neat chunks. Reserve on a plate. Halve the tomatoes, scoop out and discard some of the seeds, and add to the cucumber. Tear or chop the lettuce into bite-sized pieces.

3 Stir the dressing. Put a layer of lettuce in the bowl (do not toss), scatter in some olives and spring onion, and sprinkle in some parsley, purslane or arugula, cilantro, and mint. Add half the cucumber and tomatoes. Continue adding the ingredients until everything is in the bowl.

4 Toss the salad just before serving.

**Variation** For a spring herb salad with goat's cheese, omit the paprika, sumac, sugar, and cumin. Place half the amount of the olive oil, garlic, and lemon in a shallow bowl and mix. Top with 4 heaped tbsp each of freshly picked chervil, flat-leaf parsley, chopped spring onions, and 2 tbsp each of lemon balm, chives, and dill fronds, all chopped. Scatter over 4 tbsp of crumbled fresh goat's cheese. Toss at the last minute just before serving.

# SALAD WITH CHERVIL AND GREEN BEANS

Full of aromatic flavors and bursting with color, this salad makes a good light lunch or substantial appetizer.

**SERVES** 4 **PREP** 30 MINS **COOK** 10 MINS

14 oz (400 g) green beans, topped and tailed
sea salt and freshly ground black pepper
3 tbsp finely chopped curly parsley
2 tsp lemon thyme
1 tbsp chopped fennel fronds
2 tbsp fruity olive oil
4½ oz (125 g) arugula (or watercress)
14 oz (400 g) can artichoke hearts, drained and halved
4 slices Parma ham, torn into thin shreds

16 small black olives, pitted and chopped
4½ oz (125 g) cherry tomatoes, halved
2 spring onions, chopped
3 tbsp chopped chervil

**For the dressing**
5 tbsp fruity olive oil
sea salt and freshly ground black pepper
½ garlic clove, crushed
1½ tbsp balsamic vinegar

1 Bring a pan of lightly salted water to the boil. Add the green beans and blanch for 5–7 minutes. Refresh in cold water, and drain.

2 Place the beans in a wide shallow salad bowl. Season them lightly with salt and pepper and scatter over half the parsley, lemon thyme, and fennel. Drizzle over the olive oil, toss, and set aside.

3 Make the dressing by pouring the olive oil into a small jug. Season with salt and pepper and then whisk in the garlic and the balsamic vinegar.

4 Scatter half the arugula over the beans, then half the artichoke hearts, ham, olives, tomatoes, and spring onion. Whisk the dressing and dribble half of it over the salad. Toss gently. Add the other half of the remaining salad ingredients, except the chervil.

5 Pour on the remaining dressing. Toss, sprinkle over the chervil, and serve.

*Chervil*
*This delicate herb is perfect*
*for salads and egg dishes. Its*
*flavor vanishes if overcooked.*

# DRESSINGS AND VINAIGRETTES

Traditionally used to coat leaf salads, herby dressings are also excellent with plainly grilled fish or meats, and cooked vegetables or pulses. Mix the dressing slightly ahead of serving, but do not toss or drizzle over until the last minute.

## CHILE, CHIVE, AND GARLIC DRESSING

Try this Thai-style dressing with shrimp, chicken, or steamed vegetables.

**SERVES** 4 **PREP** 10 MINS

- 1 tbsp chopped chives
- 1 small garlic clove, crushed
- ½ small red chile, seeded and chopped
- 1 tbsp chopped cilantro
- 1 tsp fish sauce
- 2 tbsp lime juice
- 1 tsp superfine sugar
- 2fl oz (60 ml) groundnut oil

**1** Put the chives, garlic, chile, cilantro, fish sauce, lime juice, and sugar in the small bowl of a food processor. Pulse to combine.

**2** With the motor running, trickle in the groundnut oil, blending briefly until smooth. Serve soon or cover with plastic wrap and refrigerate for up to 24 hours until ready to use. Stir before using.

## MINT DRESSING

This fresh citrussy vinaigrette is wonderful on grilled lamb chops.

**SERVES** 4 **PREP** 10 MINS

- 4 tbsp chopped mint
- 2½fl oz (75 ml) fruity olive oil
- 1 tbsp freshly squeezed orange juice
- 1 tbsp lime juice
- 1 tsp fish sauce
- 1 tsp superfine sugar

**1** Put the mint in the small bowl of a food processor, and pulse to purée.

**2** Add the olive oil, orange and lime juices, fish sauce, and sugar. Blend briefly until smooth. Serve soon or cover and refrigerate for up to 24 hours until ready to use. Stir before serving.

# PARSLEY, CAPER, AND OLIVE VINAIGRETTE

Use this tangy vinaigrette on coleslaw, grilled or barbecued lamb, or shrimp.

**SERVES** 4 **PREP** 10 MINS

1 heaped tbsp chopped flat-leaf parsley
½ small garlic clove, smashed, peeled, and crushed
1 tsp dried oregano
¼ tsp superfine sugar
¼ tsp Dijon mustard
½ tbsp chopped black olives
1 tsp capers, drained
1½ tbsp balsamic vinegar
2fl oz (60 ml) fruity olive oil

**1** Put the parsley, garlic, oregano, sugar, mustard, olives, capers, and balsamic vinegar in the small bowl of a food processor, and pulse to combine.

**2** With the motor running, trickle in the olive oil, blending briefly until well mixed. Serve soon or cover and refrigerate for up to 24 hours until ready to use. If you find the sauce is a little too thick you can thin it down slightly by stirring in a splash of water. Stir well before using.

# WARM TOMATO AND GARLIC VINAIGRETTE

Dress grilled tuna, poached fish, boiled chicken, or rice with this vinaigrette.

**SERVES** 4–6 **PREP** 10 MINS **COOK** 10 MINS

3 ripe medium-large vine tomatoes
1½fl oz (45 ml) olive oil
2 garlic cloves, smashed, peeled, and crushed
¼ tsp hot paprika
1 tbsp finely chopped basil
1 tbsp finely chopped flat-leaf parsley
1 tbsp sherry vinegar
sea salt and freshly ground black pepper

**1** Place the tomatoes in a bowl, cover them with boiling water, and leave for 1 minute. Remove from water and set aside. When they are cool enough to handle, peel. Halve them and then scoop out and discard the seeds. Remove the tomato core, cut the flesh into dice, and set aside.

**2** Put the olive oil in a pan over very low heat, and add the garlic and paprika. Stir for 3–4 minutes. Add half the basil and parsley, and stir for a minute. Add the tomatoes and stir gently for 2–3 minutes until hot.

**3** Take off the heat. Stir in the reserved basil and parsley and then the sherry vinegar. Season with salt and pepper to taste and serve while still warm.

# PESTO

The famous Genoese pesto is traditionally made by patiently pounding basil and garlic with a pestle and mortar until they become a coarse scented purée into which you beat olive oil, pine nuts, and Parmesan cheese. You can make pestos with other fresh herbs, such as parsley and cilantro, and you can replace the pine nuts with fresh skinned walnuts.

## MIXED HERB PESTO

Oregano gives a nice kick to this pesto. Toss it with pasta or stir it into rice.

SERVES 2  PREP 15 MINS  COOK 20 MINS

3 tbsp coarsely chopped basil
2 tsp coarsely chopped oregano
3 tbsp coarsely chopped flat-leaf parsley
2 garlic cloves
coarse sea salt

1¾ oz (50 g) Parmesan cheese, grated
3–3½ fl oz (90–100 ml) fruity olive oil
freshly ground black pepper
10 oz (300 g) dried pasta
1 tbsp heavy cream (optional)

1 Put the herbs in a large mortar, reserving 1 tbsp to finish. Smash the garlic with the flat of a knife (see p125), peel, and add to the mortar. Sprinkle in a little salt. Pound down onto the mixture with the pestle until it is mushy.

2 Add the Parmesan a little at a time and beat vigorously to blend. Slowly beat in the olive oil until you have a thick coarse paste, and season with salt and pepper to taste.

3 Cook the pasta according to the pack instructions. Drain, reserving 2 tbsp of the cooking water. Stir the water into the pesto to loosen it slightly. Return the pasta to the hot pan and pour in the pesto. Toss to coat thoroughly. Stir in the reserved fresh herbs. If using the cream, stir it in and serve immediately.

**Cook's note** To use some of the pesto as a salad dressing, after step 3, whisk in a little balsamic or other vinegar or lemon juice. To dress a salad for 4, use 3–4 tbsp pesto and 1 tbsp balsamic vinegar.

*Oregano*
*Fresh or dried, this wonderful herb is a classic ingredient in many popular vegetable and shellfish dishes.*

# COLD SAUCES

Herbs play an essential part in flavoring cold sauces where they also help counteract fatty oil or heavy cream. Fresh herbs work the best, but dried herbs, such as mint, oregano, thyme, and marjoram, can be used ground and in small amounts.

## SAUCE VERTE

This Mediterranean favorite is particularly good with poached chicken or salmon, and with grilled tuna.

**MAKES** 8FL OZ (250 ML)  **PREP** 20 MINS

1 tbsp fresh bread crumbs made from day-old bread
1 tbsp white wine vinegar
1 tsp Dijon mustard
6fl oz (175 ml) fruity olive oil
5 tbsp finely chopped flat-leaf or curly parsley, plus stalks (optional)
3 tbsp finely chopped basil

1 tbsp finely chopped mint
2 garlic cloves, crushed
2 anchovy fillets, chopped
2 tbsp capers, drained, and finely chopped
2–3 tbsp lemon juice and 2 tsp finely grated unwaxed lemon zest
sea salt and freshly ground black pepper

1 In a bowl, mix the bread crumbs and vinegar together with the mustard and 3 tbsp of the olive oil.

2 Add the herbs (reserving 1 heaped tbsp of the mixed herbs to finish), and beat well. If you like, chop a few parsley stalks very finely and stir them in for extra flavor.

3 Add the garlic, anchovies, and half the capers, and beat again. The mixture will become a very thick green paste.

4 Gradually beat in the rest of the olive oil a little at a time and then season to taste with salt and pepper. Shortly before serving, stir in the lemon juice and zest, and add the reserved herbs and capers. Use soon or cover, chill, and use within 24 hours.

**Capers**
*Preserved capers are a versatile kitchen essential, great with oily fish and boiled meats.*

# AÏOLI

Serve this garlic mayonnaise in the traditional Provençal way—with steamed vegetables, hard-boiled eggs, and poached fish.

**MAKES** 10FL OZ (300 ML) **PREP** 20 MINS **REST** 10 MINS

2 large fresh garlic cloves, smashed and peeled
sea salt and freshly ground black pepper

1 very fresh large egg yolk
7fl oz (200 ml) mild olive oil

1 Using a pestle and mortar, pound the garlic with a small pinch of salt. Add the egg yolk and season with pepper. Beat for 1 minute and then leave to rest for 5 minutes. Beat in the oil, a few drops at a time, as for a mayonnaise.

2 Once the sauce has emulsified, pour in the olive oil in a thin trickle, beating always with the pestle in the same direction. The sauce is ready once it has a very thick texture and the pestle almost stands up by itself in the bowl.

3 Cover and refrigerate for up to 24 hours until ready to use.

# HERB MAYONNAISE

This green aromatic mayonnaise is great with asparagus, tender-stem broccoli, new potatoes, or cauliflower.

**SERVES** 4–6 **MAKES** 10FL OZ (300 ML) **PREP** 20 MINS **REST** 10 MINS

1 very fresh egg yolk
1 tsp Dijon mustard
sea salt and freshly ground black pepper
1 garlic clove, crushed
5fl oz (150 ml) vegetable oil, such as canola, groundnut, or sunflower
1 tbsp chopped basil

1 tbsp finely chopped flat-leaf parsley
1 tbsp chopped tarragon or dill fronds
½ tbsp chopped cilantro
1 sprig marjoram or oregano, leaves only
1 tbsp capers, drained
3½fl oz (100 ml) fruity olive oil
1 tbsp red wine vinegar

1 Put the egg yolk, mustard, and a little salt in the bowl of a blender or food processor. Beat with a fork. Leave to rest for 5 minutes.

2 Add the garlic and pulse a few times. With the motor running, trickle in the vegetable oil. As the mixture thickens, add the vegetable oil a little faster.

3 Once you have added all the vegetable oil, slowly feed in half the herbs and the capers. Add the olive oil, then the red wine vinegar. Stop the motor.

4 Spoon the sauce into a bowl. Taste and adjust the seasoning. Leave to rest for 5 minutes. Stir in the remaining herbs. Gradually stir in about 2 tbsp of cold water to loosen the sauce slightly. This will keep for 24 hours covered and chilled, but stir in the remaining herbs just before serving.

# CHIMICHURRI

A favorite in Argentina, this sauce is served with dishes as diverse as barbecued beef and empanadas.

**MAKES** 7–8FL OZ (200–250 ML) **PREP** 15 MINS **COOK** 15 MINS **INFUSE** 30 MINS

3½ oz (100 ml) fruity olive oil
2 garlic cloves, smashed, peeled, and crushed
2 tbsp sherry vinegar or red wine vinegar
1 shallot, finely chopped

4 tbsp chopped flat-leaf parsley
½ tsp dried marjoram or oregano
½ tsp smoked paprika
sea salt and freshly ground black pepper

**1** Whisk or beat all the ingredients except the salt and pepper together in a small bowl and then season with salt and pepper.

**2** Transfer to a clean serving bowl, cover and keep in a cool place for 2 hours before serving. Adjust the seasoning at the last minute. Chimichurri can be refrigerated for up to 48 hours.

# YOGURT SAUCE WITH PARSLEY AND MINT

Keep this soothing sauce to hand as a cooling side dish for hot spicy foods.

**MAKES** 6FL OZ (175 ML) **PREP** 20 MINS **STAND** 2 HOURS

5fl oz (150 ml) natural yogurt (not fat-free)
garlic clove, smashed, peeled, and crushed
1 tsp lemon juice
1 heaped tbsp chopped flat-leaf parsley, plus 2 tsp to finish
10 g (¼ oz) feta cheese, mashed

1 tsp chopped summer savory or marjoram
1 tsp dried mint, plus 1 tsp to finish
sea salt and freshly ground black pepper
1½ tbsp fruity olive oil, to finish

**1** Put the yogurt, garlic, lemon juice, parsley, feta cheese, savory or marjoram, and dried mint in the small bowl of a food processor. Blend until smooth. Season with salt and pepper to taste.

**2** Transfer to a bowl, cover, and keep in a cool place for 2 hours before serving. At the last minute, adjust the seasoning, and scatter over the extra parsley and mint. Drizzle over the olive oil and stir it in gently.

**Cook's note** Yogurt sauces can be refrigerated for up to 48 hours. If the sauce then looks too thick, stir in a little cold water to thin it down.

**Variations** You can vary the mixture of fresh and dried herbs, always scattering over a few extra fresh leaves just before serving. If you like, you can also replace the feta cheese with the same amount of tahini paste.

# HOT SAUCES

If you want to make the most of herbs in a hot sauce, keep the sauce simple to let the herbal flavors really come through. Melted butter, a little stock, cream, or white wine are good partners for herbs.

## FRESH SAGE SAUCE

This sauce is ideal with pork chops or tenderloin, chicken, or turkey.

MAKES 8FL OZ (250 ML) **PREP** 10 MINS **COOK** 10 MINS

2 bay leaves
4fl oz (125 ml) chicken or vegetable stock
4fl oz (125 ml) dry white wine
1 small sprig thyme
1 tbsp all-purpose flour

¾ oz (20 g) slightly softened butter, plus
½ oz (15 g) chilled butter, diced, to finish
1 tbsp chopped sage leaves, plus
3–5 small leaves to finish
sea salt and freshly ground black pepper

**1** Bruise the bay leaves with the back of a large knife or a kitchen mallet. Place in a pan over medium heat with the stock, wine, and thyme, and bring to a simmer.
**2** Mash together the flour and softened butter in a cup or on a saucer using a fork until well mixed.
**3** Whisk the butter and flour into the simmering liquid. Continue whisking for 3 minutes over a fast simmer, until the liquid has slightly thickened.
**4** Reduce the heat. Remove the bay leaves and thyme. Add the sage and stir for 2 minutes. Remove from the heat, cool for 2 minutes, and then season with salt and pepper.
**5** Whisk in the diced chilled butter, stir in the whole sage leaves, and serve.

*Sage*
*Fresh sage is unbeatable with*
*buttery risotto, while dried*
*sage is delicious in stuffings.*

# PLAIN AND SIMPLE GARLIC SAUCE

Roasted garlic makes a fragrant sauce that works wonders with roasted meats.

**MAKES** 7–8FL OZ (200–250 ML) **PREP** 15 MINS **COOK** 15 MINS **INFUSE** 30 MINS

2 heads fresh garlic, broken into unpeeled cloves
2 tbsp olive oil

5fl oz (150 ml) heavy cream
sea salt and freshly ground black pepper

1 Preheat the oven to 250°F (130°C). Put the garlic cloves on a plate, drizzle with the olive oil, and rub it all over the cloves. Line a roasting pan with foil, add the cloves, and cover loosely with foil. Place in the oven and roast for about 1 hour, until the garlic becomes very soft.
2 Take out of the oven and place the cloves onto a plate. Once cool, squeeze each clove to push out the pulp into a bowl. Mash it briefly with a fork.
3 Warm the cream in a small pan placed over low heat. Take off the heat and thoroughly whisk in the mashed garlic pulp. Season with salt and pepper to taste and reheat gently until very hot but not quite simmering. Leftover sauce can be covered and refrigerated for up to a day.

**Variations** Stir in 1 tsp ground cumin or coriander and/or 2 tsp grated root ginger. Replace the cream with the same quantity of strained full-fat yogurt, or also with stock, whisking in ¾ oz (20 g) diced chilled butter to finish off the sauce.

# MELTED BUTTER AND CHERVIL SAUCE

Make this delicate sauce at the last minute and serve with salmon, sole, asparagus, or broccoli.

**MAKES** 4FL OZ (120 ML) **PREP** 10 MINS **COOK** 15–20 MINS

1 scant tbsp cornstarch
2 oz (65 g) chilled butter, diced
2 tsp lemon juice

1 heaped tbsp finely chopped chervil
sea salt and freshly ground white pepper

1 In a pan, whisk the cornstarch with 4fl oz (120 ml) water, and season with salt. Stir over moderate heat until very hot but not boiling.
2 Whisk in the butter one piece at a time, without allowing the sauce to boil. Take off the heat and stir in the lemon juice and chervil. Season to taste with salt and white pepper and serve immediately.

**Variations** Whisk in 1 tbsp heavy cream at the last minute to make the sauce extra rich. You can also replace the chervil with the same quantity of finely chopped tarragon, dill fronds, or sorrel.

# SOUPS

Fresh and dried herbs can be used to great effect in soups, whether in a modest supporting role or as the star of the show. Use dried herbs early in the cooking and snip in plenty of fresh herbs to finish off.

## SORREL AND PEA SOUP

This smooth pea soup is given a distinctive edge with the sharp taste of sorrel.

**SERVES** 4–6 **PREP** 15 MINS **COOK** 30 MINS

I tbsp sunflower, groundnut, or canola oil
¾o z (20 g) soft butter, plus ¾o z (20 g) chilled diced butter
Ilb 2oz (500 g) shelled peas, fresh or frozen
I floury potato, peeled and cut into small dice
2 flat-leaf parsley sprigs, chopped

4 tbsp loosely packed small sorrel leaves, plus extra sorrel chopped, to garnish
sea salt and freshly ground black pepper
I¼ pints (750 ml) vegetable or chicken stock
3 tbsp heavy cream, plus extra to garnish

1 Put the oil and the soft butter in a large pan placed over a medium heat. Add the peas, potato, parsley, and half of the sorrel leaves. Stir well for 2 minutes, then reduce the heat a little. Add 3½fl oz (100 ml) water, and season lightly with salt and pepper. Partly cover and cook over very low heat, stirring occasionally, for 15 minutes until the potato is tender. Remove from the heat and let cool a little.

2 Transfer to a food processor (or use a stick blender placed directly in the pan) and blend until puréed. Return to the pan and stir in the stock. Bring to a simmer over a medium heat, stirring frequently. Reduce the heat a little and leave to simmer gently for 5 minutes. Taste, adjust the seasoning, and stir in the remaining sorrel leaves and the heavy cream.

3 Return to a low simmer, and whisk in the chilled diced butter. Adjust the seasoning and spoon into bowls. Decorate with a swirl of cream and a little chopped sorrel. Serve immediately.

***Sorrel***
*With its somewhat bitter, sour flavor, sorrel is particularly good with fish, cream, and eggs.*

# CREAM OF HERB SOUP

You can use any combination of herbs you like for this verdant soup.

**SERVES** 4 **PREP** 15 MINS **COOK** 1 HOUR

2 tbsp butter
1 oz (30 g) each chopped onion and carrots
1¾ oz (50 g) each diced celery and spring onion
¾ oz (20 g) diced parsley root
¾ oz (20 g) all-purpose flour
sea salt and freshly ground black pepper
1 liter (2 pints) chicken stock

2 garlic cloves, finely chopped
1 bay leaf
5 black peppercorns
4fl oz (120 ml) heavy cream
6 tbsp chopped herbs, such as sage, basil, parsley, chervil, sorrel, lovage, oregano, thyme, or chives, in any combination

1 Place a medium pan over low heat and add 1 tbsp butter. Add the onion, cover, and leave to sweat for about 5–10 minutes. Add the vegetables and stir to coat in butter. Cover and sweat until softened, about 5–10 minutes.
2 Sprinkle the flour over the vegetables and give them a stir. Season lightly, then pour in the stock. Raise the heat to high and bring the soup to a boil.
3 When it is boiling, turn down the heat and add the garlic, bay leaf, and peppercorns. Simmer uncovered for about 30 minutes. Skim off any froth.
4 Stir in the cream. Turn up the heat but do not boil. After 5 minutes, remove from the heat and strain the soup into a large bowl. Discard the vegetables and spices. Pour the soup back into the pan. Whisk in the rest of the butter and add the herbs, keeping some back to finish. Simmer for 5 minutes, stirring occasionally. Season to taste, spoon into bowls, and serve.

# GUACAMOLE SOUP

Creamy-textured avocados blend in well with strongly flavored herbs.

**SERVES** 4 **PREP** 15 MINS **CHILL** 1 HOUR **FINISH** 5 MINS

3 ripe Hass avocados, halved, pitted, and peeled
juice of 1 lime, plus 4 lime wedges for serving
2 tsp finely chopped lovage, plus 1 tsp to finish
2 spring onions, chopped
2 tbsp flat-leaf parsley, chopped
3 tbsp picked watercress leaves

sea salt and freshly ground black pepper
1 tsp ground cumin
1 tsp coriander seeds, crushed
1 tbsp finely chopped cilantro
1¼ pints (600 ml) light vegetable stock

1 Chop the avocados and place in the bowl of a blender or food processor. Add the lime juice, lovage, spring onion, parsley, and watercress. Season, add the cumin, coriander, and cilantro—blend briefly. Add the stock slowly with the motor running.
2 Transfer to a bowl, cover, and chill for at least 1 hour or for up to 24 hours until needed. Serve chilled, sprinkled with the reserved lovage and the lime wedges.

# TARATOR SOUP

Serve this cool, refreshing herb, yogurt, and walnut soup in chunky glasses to start a meal on a hot summer's day.

**SERVES** 4 **PREP** 20 MINS **CHILL** 2 HOURS

1 pint (475 ml) whole or two percent
  goat's or ewe's milk
3 tbsp finely chopped flat-leaf parsley
1½ tbsp finely chopped dill fronds
1½ tbsp finely chopped cilantro
2 tsp finely chopped mint
1 sprig thyme

4 tbsp fresh walnut kernels
8fl oz (250 ml) natural yogurt
small pinch of dried chile or a few drops
  Tabasco sauce
sea salt and freshly ground black pepper
small bunch of dill fronds, chopped

**1** Put the milk in a bowl, add 2 tbsp parsley, 1 tbsp each dill and cilantro, 1 tsp mint, and the thyme sprig. Stir and refrigerate for 1 hour.

**2** Put the walnuts in a pan of lightly salted boiling water, blanch for a minute, drain, crush lightly, and reserve.

**3** Remove the thyme from the milk and discard. Pour the milk and herbs into the bowl of a blender or food processor. With the motor running, add the walnuts a few at a time so they are thoroughly chopped. Then pour in the yogurt, and add the dried chile or Tabasco sauce, and blend well. Season with salt and pepper to taste. Return to the fridge for 1 hour, or even overnight, until ready to serve.

**4** To finish, stir in the reserved herbs, and the small bunch of dill fronds, and adjust the seasoning. Float in a few ice cubes and serve immediately.

**Thyme**
*One of the most useful of all
herbs, aromatic thyme is
indispensable fresh or dried.*

# TOPPINGS

Finely chopped herbs make lovely bread toppings and create wonderful fragrant crusts for baked dishes. They can also be stirred into dishes cooked on the stove top to finish them off with a fresh zingy kick.

## ROSEMARY, GARLIC, AND OLIVE TOPPING

For another scented bread, replace the rosemary with thyme, or 2 tbsp mixed anise seed or fennel seeds, and use sun-dried tomatoes instead of olives.

FOR 1¾ LB (800 G) DOUGH  **SERVES** 8–10  **PREP** 20 MINS  **REST** 30 MINS  **COOK** 25–30 MINS

3½ fl oz (100 ml) fruity olive oil
6 garlic cloves, peeled and cut into slivers
1 lb 2oz (500 g) pack white bread mix
16 black olives, pitted and chopped

5 stalks rosemary, about 3 in (7.5 cm) long, leaves stripped, stalks discarded
coarse sea salt and freshly ground black pepper

1 Put paper towels onto a plate. Pour the olive oil into a pan over low heat. Add the garlic. Cook for 2 minutes until softened but not colored. Lift out the garlic and spread it on the paper towels. Let the oil and garlic cool.

2 Make bread according to package instructions. When it is ready, knock the air out of it. Spread the dough into an oiled 12 x 8 in (30 x 22 cm) baking tray and flatten gently.

3 Drizzle 1 tbsp of the cold garlicky oil over the dough, and spread it round. Scatter over the garlic, olives, and rosemary and pat in lightly. Drizzle over 1–2 tbsp of the oil. Cover loosely with plastic wrap and let rest for 30 minutes.

4 Preheat the oven to 375°F (190°C). Remove the plastic wrap and place the tray in the oven. Bake for 20–25 minutes. Let cool, season, and drizzle over the remaining oil.

## MANAKEISH

This fragrant lemony topping for bread is popular in the Middle East.

FOR 1¾ LB (800 G) DOUGH  **SERVES** 8–10  **PREP** 20 MINS  **REST** 30 MINS  **COOK** 25–30 MINS

3 tbsp lemon thyme
1 tsp ground sumac
1 tsp dried mint
2 garlic cloves, crushed

1 tbsp coarsely grated lemon zest
1 tbsp lemon juice
5 tbsp fruity olive oil
1 lb 2oz (500 g) pack white bread mix

1 Pound, mash, or blend all the topping ingredients together.

2 Make bread according to the package instructions. When it is ready, knock the air out of it. Spread the dough into an oiled 12 x 8 in (30 x 22 cm) baking tray and flatten gently.

3 Spread the topping over the bread, leave to rest, and bake as above.

# SWEET IDEAS

Many herbs, especially mint, basil, and cilantro, add a lovely distinctive note to custards, syrups, and fruit desserts. Use in small amounts: too little is better than too much as the aromatic strength of herbs can easily overpower a delicate sweet concoction.

## BASIL AND VANILLA CUSTARD

**Drizzle this infused custard over strawberry tarts, crumbles, and fruit snacks.**

**SERVES** 4–6 **PREP** 20 MINS **COOK** 30 MINS PLUS COOLING

- 16fl oz (500 ml) whole milk
- 3 tbsp loosely packed basil leaves, plus a few small leaves to decorate
- 2 vanilla pods
- 3 large or 4 medium fresh egg yolks
- 6 tbsp superfine sugar
- 1 tsp cornstarch
- 3 tbsp crème fraîche
- Szechuan pepper (optional), to garnish

1 Put the milk in a pan. Squash the basil leaves with your hands, and add them to the milk. Split the vanilla pods lengthwise and scrape out the black pulpy seeds. Put the pods and seeds in the pan. Bring to a simmer over a low heat, stirring occasionally with a wooden spoon. As soon as the milk starts to bubble, reduce the heat as low as possible, and cook very gently, stirring frequently, for 10 minutes. Take off the heat and set aside.

2 In a large bowl, whisk together the egg yolks and the sugar until smooth and pale. Whisk in the cornstarch.

3 Place a fine sieve over the bowl, and strain the hot milk a little at a time into the yolk and sugar mixture. Push down the basil and vanilla into the sieve to extract as much flavor as possible. Whisk the yolk mixture well between additions. Discard the vanilla pod and basil after sieving.

4 Return the mixture to the pan over very low heat. Bring to a gentle simmer, stirring constantly for 10 minutes or until the custard has thickened enough to coat the back of the spoon. Do not allow it to boil. If necessary take it off the heat from time to time.

5 Leave to get cold, stirring occasionally. Stir in the crème fraîche and once the custard is completely cold, place it in the fridge to chill further.

6 Serve well chilled, decorated with small basil leaves. If you like, you can grind a little Szechuan pepper over the custard before serving to bring out the mild pepperiness of the basil.

# MINT AND ORANGE SYRUP

This syrup is lovely for flavoring juleps, cocktails, sangria, and wine cups.

**MAKES** 250ML (8FL OZ) **PREP** 15 MINS **COOK** 20 MINS

5 tbsp chopped mint, preferably Moroccan mint
grated zest from 1–2 large unwaxed oranges
10 oz (300 g) superfine sugar

3½fl oz (100 ml) freshly squeezed orange juice
2 tbsp Cointreau or other orange liqueur

You will need: 2 pieces of clean **cheesecloth**, dampened; **string**; fine **sieve**; **funnel**; sterilized 8fl oz (250 ml) **bottle or jar** (see p176) with a stopper or lid

1 Put the mint and grated orange zest in a double layer of cheesecloth, bring up the edges, and tie with string (see p129). Put the sugar, orange juice, orange liqueur, and 7fl oz (200 ml) water in a pan, and add the cheesecloth bag.
2 Bring to a boil over moderate heat, stirring occasionally until the sugar has dissolved. Leave to simmer for 5–7 minutes, stirring from time to time until the syrup has thickened just a little.
3 Remove from the heat, cover, and leave to get cool. Lift out the cheesecloth bag and squeeze it over the pan to extract as much flavor as possible, then discard it. Strain the syrup through a fine sieve lined with dampened cheesecloth into a sterilized bottle and seal. Store in a cool place and use within 4–6 weeks.

# LAVENDER SYRUP

Try with baked apples, roasted apricots, poached peaches, and creamy yogurt.

**MAKES** 7–8FL OZ (200–250 ML) **PREP** 15 MINS **COOK** 15 MINS **INFUSE** 30 MINS

2 tsp dried lavender flowers
10 oz (300 g) superfine sugar

pared zest of 1 small unwaxed lemon, cut into small strips

You will need: piece of clean **cheesecloth**, dampened; fine **sieve; funnel**; sterilized 8fl oz (250 ml) **bottle or jar** (see p178) with a stopper or lid

1 Put the dried lavender flowers, sugar, and lemon zest strips into a saucepan with 10fl oz (300 ml) water. Place over medium heat and stir.
2 Once the sugar has dissolved after 3–4 minutes, stop stirring and remove from the heat. Leave to infuse for at least 30 minutes, stirring occasionally.
3 Place the pan over medium heat and bring to a boil without stirring. Turn the heat to high and let bubble for 5–7 minutes until thickened.
4 Remove from heat. When the syrup is cool enough to handle, strain carefully into a sterilized bottle through a fine sieve lined with dampened cheesecloth. Leave to cool completely, seal, and store in a cool place. Use within 4–6 weeks.

# CORDIALS

The delicate flavors of herbs make wonderful, refreshing cordials, which you can enjoy long after the growing season. Always use scrupulously clean utensils to minimize the risk of fermentation.

## BLACK CURRANT CORDIAL

A couple of tablespoons of this cordial added to a glass of sparkling mineral water makes a perfect summer's day thirst quencher.

**MAKES** 1⅔ PINTS (800 ML)  **PREP** 20 MINS

1lb (450 g) black currants
8oz (225 g) sugar

zest and juice of 1 well-washed unwaxed lemon

You will need: piece of clean **cheesecloth**, dampened; **funnel**; sterilized 1¾ pint (1 liter) **bottle or jar** (see p176) with a stopper or lid

1 Place the black currants, sugar, and 8fl oz (250 ml) water in a pan over low heat. Bring to a simmer, stirring occasionally. Gently mash the black currants to make sure that all of the berries have broken open. Cook for 5–8 minutes, until the sugar has dissolved and the black currants have yielded their juice.
2 Stir in the lemon juice and zest and remove the pan from the heat.
3 Slowly strain the contents of the pan through a funnel lined with dampened cheesecloth into a sterilized bottle. Allow the liquid to cool, then seal and refrigerate. Use within 6–8 weeks.

***Black currants***
*Packed with vitamin C,
black currants are
great for cordials.*

## ELDERFLOWER CORDIAL

Either dilute this fragrant cordial in sparkling mineral water, or use as a flavoring in ice cream or other sweet dishes.

**MAKES** 1⅔ PINTS (800 ML) **PREP** 20 MINS **INFUSE** 48 HOURS

1 lb (450 g) sugar
2 unwaxed lemons, well washed

15 large elderflower heads in full flower, shaken to dislodge any insects
½ oz (15 g) citric acid

You will need: piece of clean **cheesecloth**, dampened; **sieve; funnel**; sterilized 1¾ pint (1 liter) **bottle or jar** (see below) with a stopper or lid

1 Place the sugar in a large bowl and pour 1¼ pints (600 ml) boiling water over it. Stir until the sugar dissolves, then set aside.
2 Grate the zest from the lemons and add to the sugar water. Then slice the lemons thickly and add them to the sugar water as well.
3 Submerge the elderflower heads in the sugar water and lemon mixture. Add the citric acid and stir to dissolve. Cover and set aside for 48 hours to infuse.
4 Line a sieve with a piece of dampened cheesecloth and set over a large bowl. Carefully filter the cordial through the sieve. Place a funnel into the neck of a sterilized bottle and slowly pour the cordial into it. Seal the lid and store in a cool, dark place. Once opened, store in the fridge for up to 3 weeks.

**To sterilize bottles and jars,** preheat the oven to 250°F (130°C). Wash the bottles or jars in soapy water. Rinse well, and then drain. Place upright in the oven for 15 minutes before using. You can also sterilize glass containers by running them through a hot cycle of the dishwasher.

*Elderflower*
*Floral-scented elderflowers*
*make the most refreshing*
*cordials when pure white.*

# ANGELICA LIQUEUR

**Vodka absorbs the flavor of the herbs in this spicy liqueur that packs a punch.**

**MAKES** 12FL OZ (360 ML)  **PREP** 30 MINS  **INFUSE** 3–6 MONTHS

2 cardamom seeds, crushed
1 tsp dried marjoram, crumbled
pinch each of ground allspice, ground star anise,
  ground cinnamon, and ground coriander
12fl oz (360 ml) vodka

4fl oz (120 ml) sugar syrup using 5½ oz
  (60 g) sugar to 2¾ fl oz (80 ml) water
2 tbsp finely chopped angelica root,
  washed and thoroughly dried

You will need: piece of clean **cheesecloth**, dampened; **sieve**; sterilized 1¼ pint (600 ml) **jar** with a lid, 1 small sterilized **jar** with a lid, plus 1 sterilized decorative 1¼ pint (600 ml) **bottle** (see opposite) with stopper

1 Crush the cardamom in a mortar and pestle and place in the larger sterilized jar. Add the marjoram, allspice, star anise, cinnamon, and coriander. Pour in 4 tbsp of the vodka. Seal and store in a cool dark place for 7 days.

2 After 7 days, filter the mixture through a sieve lined with dampened cheesecloth into a bowl. Add the sugar syrup and 8fl oz of the vodka. Re-sterilize the jar, add the liqueur mixture, and close the lid. Set aside in a cool, dark place for 2 weeks.

3 In a separate small sterilized jar with a lid, place the chopped angelica root and add the remaining 4 tbsp of vodka. Close the lid tightly and store in a cool, dark place. After 2 weeks, strain the liquid as before, pressing down gently on the angelica root. Add the angelica extract to the herb-spice liqueur by ½ teaspoons until you achieve the flavor you like.

4 Store the remaining angelica extract, if any, and the liqueur in their closed jars in a cool, dark place for 2 months, then taste the liqueur. Add more angelica extract if you like. Pour into a sterilized decorative bottle, close tightly, and store for 3 more months for the best developed flavor.

*Angelica*
*To dry angelica root, cut it into*
*long strips and dry overnight in*
*the oven on a very low heat.*

# HERBAL TEAS

There's something immensely satisfying about making herbal teas using herbs or seeds you have grown and harvested yourself. Herbal teas are regarded by some as nature's medicine and there is no denying the power of a cup of herbal tea to relax or uplift you, depending on the herb you choose.

## MAKING TEA

After harvesting your herbs give them a rinse, blot them on a paper towel, then chop them finely (see p123). To use your own dried herbs, see p114. Here is a general guide for making herbal tea.

**1** You will need either 2 tbsp of finely chopped fresh herbs or 1 tbsp of finely crumbled dried herbs for every cup of tea you wish to make. Place in a teapot.

**2** Bring enough water to boil to fill your cups. The instant the water reaches a boil, pour it on the herbs. Water boiled for too long makes flat-tasting tea.

**3** Steep the herbs in the teapot for 5 minutes. If you want your tea to be stronger, use more herbs rather than a longer steeping time.

**4** Warm the tea cups by running them under hot water for a few moments, and empty them. Then pour the tea through a strainer into the cups.

**5** You can add 1 tsp of honey or sugar, or a squeeze of lemon to flavor the tea to taste, or serve it without any additional ingredients. Ideally, the tea cups or tea pot should be non-metallic. Enamelled metal will do, but glass is better. Very best of all are ceramic or porcelain tea cups and teapots.

## ICED TEA

Coldness dulls the palate, so make your iced tea about one-third stronger than your ordinary cup of hot herbal tea, and allow the tea to cool before adding it to the ice cubes. Use herbs with mint and lemon flavors, such as spearmint and lemongrass, to create extra refreshing cold drinks.

**1** Make enough herbal tea to freeze some in ice cube trays while the rest chills in the fridge. Using herbal tea ice cubes in your iced tea avoids diluting the tea.

**2** Once they have frozen solid (after about 2 hours) pop the herbal tea ice cubes out of the tray and place them in a tall glass. Pour over the cooled herbal tea.

**3** Garnish your iced tea with a fresh sprig of the same herb you used to make the tea. You can also add slices of lemon, lime, or orange.

### MAKING A DECOCTION

A decoction is used for tougher herbs, such as juniper berries and angelica root. Pour 16fl oz (500 ml) of water into a pan and add 2–4 heaped tsp of chopped, crushed, or grated herbs. Bring to a boil, cover, and reduce the heat. Simmer for 20 minutes, turn off the heat, and steep for 10 minutes. Strain and serve, or refrigerate in a sealed jar for 1 week.

## HOW TO MAKE TEA BAGS

The great advantage of making tea bags using herbs you've grown and dried yourself (see p114) is that you can control the quality and the taste. Make the tea bags as you need them, or prepare them ahead of time. When used in tea, dried herbs are about twice as potent as fresh herbs.

**1** Take the dried herb of your choice out of its storage jar and gently crumble the leaves or flower heads. Use a single herb, or create your own blend of herbs.

**2** Cut a 4 x 4 in (10 x 10 cm) cheesecloth square. Place 1 tbsp of dried herbs in the middle of it. This will be enough for a single cup of herbal tea.

**3** Bring up the corners of the cheesecloth to enclose the dried herbs. Hold the corners together and tie them securely with a piece of kitchen string.

**4** Place the bag in the cup and pour on the boiling water. Allow the tea to steep for five minutes, or until it suits your taste, remove the tea bag, and serve.

# MOROCCAN MINT TEA

This sweet mint tea accompanies most meals all across North Africa, not just in Morocco. Its ubiquity doesn't detract from its delicacy.

### SERVES 8

3 tbsp loose green tea or 5 tea bags of green tea
1 bunch fresh Moroccan mint or spearmint
3½ pints (1½ liters) water
7 oz (200 g) superfine sugar

1 Place the green tea and fresh mint into a large teapot.
2 Pour the water into a large pan over high heat. Bring to boiling, then pour it carefully into the teapot. Steep for 5 minutes, stirring gently once or twice. Add the sugar and stir until it dissolves.
3 Pour the hot tea through a strainer into serving cups, or cool and pour over ice cubes in glasses for iced mint tea.

# ROSEHIP TEA

During World War II, when oranges from the continent were scarce, British schoolchildren were given rosehip syrup for their daily dose of vitamin C. The tea is light and tangy.

### SERVES 2

7 large hips of *Rosa rugosa*, stems removed
16fl oz (480 ml) water

1 Coarsely chop the rosehips, including the seeds, and place in a teapot.
2 Pour the water into a pan over high heat or into a kettle and bring to boiling. Pour over the rosehips.
3 Steep for 10 minutes, strain, and serve in warmed cups.

# ENGLISH VIOLET TEA

This was a great favorite in Britain during the reign of Queen Victoria. Float a fresh English violet in each cup for extra flavor and a charming garnish.

### SERVES 3

18 English violets, picked over and gently rinsed
1¼ pints (600 ml) water

1 Place the English violets in a teapot.
2 Pour the water into a pan over high heat or into a kettle and bring to boiling. Immediately pour it into the teapot and stir gently.
3 Steep for 10 minutes and then pour through a strainer into warmed cups.

# CHAMOMILE TEA

One of the most popular herbal teas in the world today, chamomile was enjoyed by the ancient Egyptians and early Romans. It is both relaxing and reviving.

**SERVES** 3

3 heaped tbsp fresh chamomile flowers
1¼ pints (600 ml) water
honey to taste (optional)

**1** Place the chamomile flowers in a teapot.
**2** Pour the water into a pan over high heat or into a kettle and bring to boiling. Immediately pour into the teapot. Steep for 5–10 minutes.
**3** Pour the tea through a strainer into warmed cups. Add honey to taste and stir, or drink it unsweetened.

# TILLEUL TEA

Europe's famous linden tree (*Tilia europaea*) is also known as the lime tree. Its flowers make a delightful, relaxing tea with a light, floral scent.

**SERVES** 3

9 linden flowers
1¼ pints (600 ml) water
1½ tsp honey

**1** Place the linden flowers in a teapot.
**2** Pour the water into a pan over high heat or into a kettle and bring to boiling. Immediately pour it into the teapot and add the honey.
**3** Steep for 5 minutes, then strain into warmed cups.

# FOUR-HERB DIGESTIF TEA

A digestif is, as you can tell by its name, an aid to digestion. Here's one to make straight from your own herb garden. This keeps in the fridge for up to 6 days.

**SERVES** 4

2 tbsp each peppermint, fennel fronds, lemon balm, and chamomile flowers, roughly chopped
1¾ pints (800 ml) water
honey to taste (optional)

**1** Place the chopped herbs in a teapot.
**2** Pour the water into a pan over high heat or into a kettle and bring to boiling. Immediately pour it into the teapot.
**3** Steep for 10 minutes, then strain into warmed cups.

## LAVENDER AND LEMON VERBENA TEA

Lemon verbena on its own makes a lovely, lemony tea, but when it is paired with the floral scent of lavender, something special happens.

SERVES 6

5 oz (140 g) lemon verbena leaves, loosely torn
3 tbsp lavender flower heads
2¾ pints (1.3 liters) water

1 Tear up the lemon verbena leaves and place in a bowl. Add the lavender flower heads and stir to mix. Place in a large teapot. (For a single serving of tea, use 1 tsp of each herb in a cup.)
2 Pour the water into a pan over high heat and bring to a boil, then pour it into the teapot (or cup). Steep for 5 minutes.
3 Pour through a strainer into warmed cups (for a single cup, strain into another cup).

## SAGE AND LEMON BALM TEA

By itself, sage has a rather strong, herbaceous flavor, which is much more palatable when combined with lemon balm.

SERVES 2

2 tbsp sage, finely chopped
3 tbsp lemon balm, finely chopped

16fl oz (480ml) water
1 tsp honey

1 Place the sage and lemon balm in a teapot.
2 Pour the water into a pan over high heat or into a kettle and bring to a boil. Immediately pour it into the teapot. Add the honey and stir. Steep for 10-15 minutes.
3 Pour the tea through a strainer into warmed cups.

## FRESH GINGER TEA

This is a favorite tea during the cold and flu season but it's reviving any time.

SERVES 4

2 in (5 cm) fresh root ginger, peeled and
  thinly sliced
1¾ pints (1 liter) water

1 tsp honey
4 lemon slices

1 Bring the water just to a boil in a pan over high heat. Add the ginger slices, cover, and reduce the heat. Simmer for 15 minutes.
2 Add the honey and stir to dissolve.
3 Strain into warmed cups, add a slice of lemon to each, and serve.

# BERGAMOT TEA

The leaves and flowers of bergamot have a citrus fragrance and flavor. Bergamot tea with a squeeze of lemon makes refreshing iced tea.

**SERVES** 3

2 tbsp bergamot leaves and flowers, finely chopped
1¼ pints (600 ml) water

honey to taste
3 lemon slices

**1** Place the bergamot leaves and flowers in a teapot.
**2** Pour the water into a pan over high heat or into a kettle and bring to a boil. Immediately pour it into the teapot. Stir in a little honey to taste.
**3** Steep for 5–10 minutes. Pour through a strainer into warmed cups. Garnish each cup with a slice of lemon.

# ANISE HYSSOP AND CALAMINT TEA

Anise hyssop and calamint each make delightful teas on their own, but together play strongly on the minty theme with a light note of liquorice in the background.

**SERVES** 3

1 tbsp anise hyssop, finely chopped
1 tbsp calamint leaves and stem, finely chopped

1¼ pints (600 ml) water
honey to taste

**1** Place the herbs in a teapot.
**2** Pour the water into a pan over high heat or into a kettle and bring to a boil. Immediately pour it into the teapot. Add a little honey to taste. Steep for 5 minutes or longer if you like it stronger.
**3** Pour through a strainer into warmed cups.

# ROSE-SCENTED GERANIUM TEA

This tea has long been used as a calming and stress-relieving drink. Other scented geranium leaves can also be used to make different teas.

**SERVES** 4

6½ oz (185 g) rose-scented geranium leaves
1¾ pints (1 liter) water
honey to taste

**1** Place the leaves in a teapot.
**2** Pour the water into a pan over high heat or into a kettle and bring to a boil. Immediately pour it into the teapot. Add honey to taste and stir.
**3** Steep for 5 minutes, strain into warmed cups, and serve.

# PARTNER CHARTS

Some herb and ingredient marriages—fennel and sea bass, basil and tomato, and egg and tarragon—are made in heaven. Others are less obvious but also exciting. These charts guide you to some different combinations worth trying.

## MEAT

| INGREDIENT | HERB PARTNERS | COOK'S NOTES |
|---|---|---|
| Beef | *Bouquet garni, Parsley, Bay leaf, Thyme, Lovage, Juniper berries, Holy basil, Horseradish, Orange, Chile, Garlic, Green onion, Capers, Caraway seeds* | *A generous bouquet garni tied together with dried orange peel works wonders in slow-cooked beef dishes* |
| Lamb, mutton | *Rosemary, Lemon, Lime, Garlic, Basil, Lavender, Capers, Cilantro, Mint, Fennel* | *Go easy on the rosemary with spring lamb; chop fresh mint and cilantro and add to pan juices after roasting lamb* |
| Pork | *Garlic, Fennel seeds, Thyme, Sage, Parsley, Hyssop, Bay leaf, Curry leaf, Cilantro, Marjoram, Bergamot, Holy Basil, Caraway seeds* | *Use crushed fennel seeds with pork belly; before roasting, insert sage leaves and garlic slivers into cuts made in meat* |
| Veal | *Sage, Bay leaf, Parsley, Thyme, Savory, Capers, Lemon, Orange, Garlic, Lemon balm, Caraway seeds* | *Top osso bucco (veal casserole) with gremolata; use fresh thyme or savory for delicately poached veal blanquette* |
| Venison, furred game | *Bay leaf, Juniper berries, Fennel, Rosemary, Sage, Thyme, Parsley, Hyssop* | *Add plenty of mixed herbs to marinades for venison* |

## POULTRY

| INGREDIENT | HERB PARTNERS | COOK'S NOTES |
|---|---|---|
| Chicken, poussin, turkey | *Parsley, Garlic, Chives, Bouquet garni, Tarragon, Dill, Smallage, Thyme, Lemon, Fennel, Sage, Chervil, Lime, Bergamot, Holy basil, Pot marigold* | *Be generous—poultry can be on the bland side and responds well to aromatic assistance* |
| Duck | *Parsley, Garlic, Bouquet garni, Chives, Tarragon, Dill, Smallage, Thyme, Lemon, Orange* | |
| Goose | *Parsley, Garlic, Bouquet garni, Tarragon, Dill, Smallage, Thyme, Lemon, Bay leaf* | *Dried thyme is particularly good with goose fat* |
| Guinea fowl, pheasant, wild birds | *Parsley, Garlic, Chives, Bouquet garni, Tarragon, Dill, Smallage, Thyme, Lemon, Hyssop* | |

# FISH AND SHELLFISH

| INGREDIENT | HERB PARTNERS | COOK'S NOTES |
|---|---|---|
| Cod, mahi mahi, catfish, tilapia, monkfish | *Dill, Parsley, Thyme, Bay leaf, Sorrel, Lemon, Horseradish, Lemon basil, Pot marigold, Perilla, Sage, Rosemary* | *You can be a little more generous with thyme and parsley when flavoring a mild-tasting fish, such as catfish* |
| Salmon, trout, skate, eel | *Dill, Parsley, Bay leaf, Capers, Orange, Lemon, Fennel, Horseradish, Lemon basil, Rosemary* | *Capers, butter, and a splash of wine vinegar are a classic accompaniment for skate* |
| Sardines, mackerel, tuna, herring | *Dill, Parsley, Sorrel, Arugula, Fennel, Lemon* | *Scatter plenty of herbs over fish before grilling, roasting, or pan-frying* |
| Sea bass, sea bream | *Fennel, Cilantro, Lemongrass, Lemon, Lemon basil* | *Stuff plenty of herbs inside the cavity before roasting* |
| Sole, turbot, plaice, halibut | *Parsley, Lemon, Lemon basil* | *The delicate flavor of these fish only requires a little parsley, lemon, and butter* |
| Goatfish, Mediterranean fish | *Fennel, Parsley, Lemon, Orange, Lemon basil, Pot marigold* | |
| Mussels, clams, oysters | *Parsley, Garlic, Chives, Thyme, Fennel, Dill* | *Steam mussels in white wine flavored with finely chopped mixed herbs* |
| Shrimp, crab, lobster, squid | *Garlic, Ginger, Chives, Lemongrass, Cilantro, Chile, Parsley, Lime, Oregano* | |

# DAIRY

| INGREDIENT | HERB PARTNERS | COOK'S NOTES |
|---|---|---|
| Eggs | *Parsley, Tarragon, Chervil, Dill, Chives, Green onion, Wild garlic, Thyme, Savory, Sweet cicely, Marjoram, Sorrel* | *Use finely chopped fresh fines herbes to flavor eggs; a little thyme or savory is good with a robust omelet* |
| Cheese: | | *Fresh, creamy cheeses respond well to finely chopped fines herbes; mature cheeses to a sprinkling of dried seeds; and cooked cheese to mustard seeds* |
| Fresh, creamy | *Basil, Sage, Chives, Lemon balm, Marjoram* | |
| Semi-hard, hard | *Cumin seeds, Fennel seeds, Caraway seeds, Coriander seeds, Mustard seeds* | |
| Yogurt, cream | *Parsley, Tarragon, Chervil, Dill, Chives, Mint, Cilantro, Borage, Sorrel* | *Mix equal parts water and yogurt with ice cubes and finely chopped cilantro, parsley, or chives for a refreshing drink* |

# VEGETABLES, LEGUMES, AND WHEAT

| INGREDIENT | HERB PARTNERS | COOK'S NOTES |
|---|---|---|
| Sweet peppers, eggplant, zucchini | *Garlic, Chile, Parsley, Cilantro, Tarragon, Dill, Oregano, Marjoram* | *Raw or grilled zucchini are good with fresh tarragon and dill* |
| Spinach | *Garlic, Chile, Lemon* | *Stir-fry and squeeze lemon over* |
| Cabbage, cauliflower, broccoli, broccoli rabe, Brussels sprouts | *Parsley, Thyme, Savory, Garlic, Juniper berries, Capers, Fennel seeds, Coriander seeds, Caraway seeds, Bay leaf* | *Slow-cooked red cabbage and cured sauerkraut are particularly good with fennel seeds, coriander seeds, capers, and juniper berries* |
| Green beans | *Garlic, Parsley, Chervil, Cilantro* | |
| Asian green vegetables | *Garlic, Ginger, Ground coriander, Chives, Chile, Cumin, Lemongrass* | |
| Celery | *Coriander seeds, Chives, Parsley* | |
| Salad leaves | *Fines herbes* | *Do not use with dried herbs* |
| Mushrooms | *Garlic, Parsley, Chives, Dill, Cilantro* | |
| Beets | *Parsley, Chives, Cilantro, Thyme* | *Use fresh herbs for boiled beets; dried thyme for roasted beets* |
| Carrots | *Garlic, Sage, Cumin, Bay leaf, Thyme, Dill, Fennel* | |
| Potatoes | *Garlic, Garlic chives, Wild garlic, Chives, Parsley, Thyme, Bay leaf, Rosemary, Sage, Dill, Mint, Chervil, Fines herbes* | *Use chopped fines herbes, dill, or mint on new potatoes; garlic, thyme, and Mediterranean herbs on roasted potatoes* |
| Sweet potatoes | *Garlic, Rosemary, Thyme, Bay leaf, Fennel seeds* | |
| Rutabaga, parsnips, turnips, squashes | *Parsley, Thyme, Rosemary, Garlic* | *Roasted vegetables thrive on garlic and strongly flavored Mediterranean herbs* |
| Globe artichokes | *Chervil, Parsley, Garlic, Chives, Mint, Lovage, Smallage, Dill, Sorrel* | *Serve with a garlicky vinaigrette* |
| Peas | *Chervil, Parsley, Chives, Mint, Lovage, Smallage, Dill, Sorrel, Savory* | |
| Beans (fava, dried, lima), chickpeas | *Bouquet garni, Savory, Garlic, Parsley, Lovage, Mint, Cilantro, Bay leaf, Thyme, Marjoram, Oregano, Good King Henry, Cumin, Arugula* | *Drain beans after cooking with bouquet garni, then scatter with fresh herbs* |
| Lentils | *Garlic, Green onion, Parsley, Thyme, Bay leaf, Cilantro, Savory* | *Finely chopped parsley is good with green lentils* |
| Bulgur wheat | *Cilantro, Garlic, Parsley, Thyme, Mint* | *Add chopped herbs generously* |

# FRUIT

Use herbs in moderation, as they can easily overpower the fragile flavor of fruit

| INGREDIENT | HERB PARTNERS | COOK'S NOTES |
|---|---|---|
| Tomatoes | Basil, Marjoram, Oregano, Lovage, Tarragon, Cilantro, Garlic, Chives | Tomato and tarragon is as good as tomato and basil |
| Avocados | Chives, Arugula, Lovage, Smallage, Sorrel, Cilantro | |
| Apples | Lavender, Cilantro, Fennel | |
| Pears | Rosemary, Lavender, Cilantro | Use dried herbs very sparingly |
| Bananas | Lemon, Orange, Mint, Cilantro, Lemongrass | |
| Peaches, nectarines, apricots, plums | Basil, Sweet cicely, Cilantro, Lavender | Fresh herbs work better with poached fruit; use dried cilantro and lavender in dried fruit compotes |
| Grapes | Cilantro, Lemon | |
| Berries, cherries | Chocolate mint, Basil | Chocolate mint is lovely with raspberries; try chopped basil and a sprinkling of balsamic vinegar with strawberries |
| Melon | Mint, Basil, Cilantro | |
| Rhubarb | Orange, Sweet cicely, Ginger | Cook in orange-scented sugar |
| Mangoes, pineapples, papayas, kiwi | Lemon, Mint, Basil, Cilantro | Sprinkle grated citrus zest and finely chopped basil over sliced fruit |
| Citrus fruits | Lemongrass, Cilantro | |
| Coconut | Chile, Ginger, Garlic, Chives, Cilantro, Thai basil | Herbs counteract the fattiness of coconut in cooked dishes |
| Figs | Cilantro, Lavender | |

# DESSERTS AND SWEET THINGS

| INGREDIENT | HERB PARTNERS | COOK'S NOTES |
|---|---|---|
| Pastries, cookies, cakes | Dill seeds, Fennel seeds, Coriander seeds, Caraway seeds, Ginger, Lavender | |
| Custards, cream, ice cream | Bay leaf, Lavender, Cilantro, Sweet cicely, Elder, Angelica, Chocolate mint, Cinnamon basil | Put the herbs in a cheesecloth bag and infuse custard the milk |
| Chocolate | Ginger, Mint, Orange, Cilantro, Lemongrass, Lemon, Fennel seeds, Rose petals | Use aromatic flavors sparingly with good quality chocolate |

# INDEX

# ACKNOWLEDGMENTS

**Dorling Kindersley** would like to thank Helena Caldon and Constance Novis for their editing, William Reavell, Peter Anderson, and Sarah Ashun for the beautiful photography, Nicky Collings for directing the photography, Alison Shackleton for the use of her garden, Jan Stevens, Bren Parkins-Knight, and Anna Burges-Lumsden for their recipe testing, Jane Lawrie for her food styling, Victoria Allen for prop styling, Mandy Earey for her design assistance, Lucy Boyd, Helen Kells, and Charlotte Senn at Petersham Nurseries for their stunning herb plantings, Emma Callery and Kajal Mistry for their editorial help, Sue Morony for proof-reading, Hilary Bird for creating the index, Romaine Werblow for her picture research, and the following for their herbs: Arne Herbs, Jekka's Herb Farm, The Perennial Nursery, Cotswold Garden Flowers, Plants4Presents, and Highdown Nursery.

**Jeff Cox** I would like to acknowledge and thank my herbal mentors: Lamar Bumbaugh, who showed me where the ginseng grows; Cyrus Hyde of Wellsweep Herb Farm, who increased my general knowledge of herbs; and especially the great chefs of Sonoma County, California, who continue to show me how to use the culinary herbs to tasty advantage. Thanks to all at DK and to Helena Caldon for her editing prowess.

**Mary-Pierre Moine** Thanks to the DK team and in particular Andrew Roff, Constance Novis, and Helena Caldon for their thoroughness, tact, and sense of humor. I'd also like to thank Philippa Davenport who helped my herb gardens over the years by giving me my first plot of sorrel, and my latest cutting of lovage.

All images © Dorling Kindersley
For further information see: www.dkimages.com